Goal Power

A Real Life Girls' Soccer Story

Mandy Cross

ELEMENT
CHILDREN'S BOOKS

SHAFTESBURY, DORSET · BOSTON, MASSACHUSETTS · MELBOURNE, VICTORIA

© Element Children's Books 1999
Text © Mandy Cross 1999
Illustrations © Paddy Mounter 1999

First published in Great Britain in 1999 by
Element Children's Books
Shaftesbury, Dorset SP7 8BP

Published in the USA in 1999 by
Element Books, Inc.
160 North Washington Street,
Boston MA 02114

Published in Australia in 1999 by
Element Books and distributed by
Penguin Australia Limited,
487 Maroondah Highway, Ringwood,
Victoria 3134

Cover design by Mandy Sherliker.
Cover photograph by Helen Marsden Photography.
Typeset by Dorchester Typesetting Group Ltd.
Printed and bound in Great Britain by Creative Print and Design.

British Library Cataloguing in Publication data available.
Library of Congress Cataloging in Publication data available.

ISBN 1 902618 46 7

Contents

AMAZON VILLA

Me (Holly)

Della

Denise

Cassy

Antonella

Nina

CHAPTER ONE

GIRLS CAN'T PLAY

She knew right after the third missed challenge.

For the first, she was faced with a defender when the ball broke in her direction. She stepped left towards it, set to take it inside. Instead, a sudden pirouette took her right, throwing her marker. She let the ball roll across in front of her, nudged it with her right foot around the defender – whose boots seemed glued to the ground – and skipped outside him.

A second defender charged over, committing himself way too early, leaving a gap on his inside wide enough for a sumo wrestler to waltz through. She darted past him, picking up speed. Deft touches on the ball kept it perfectly under control in front of her, just as her father had taught her.

Another opponent quickly came in to challenge, and he seemed to know what he was doing. Backing off, keeping himself between her and the goal, he was checking her run. She dropped her right shoulder, then veered left, taking the ball with the outside of her left boot. It shouldn't have been enough, but the defender just fell away out of her path, and that's when she knew. Holly Kerrigan, the only girl among the 32 soccer-mad youngsters attending the Soccer Fun summer coaching course, was being set up.

"Oh yeah," Holly called out, trapping the ball with the sole of her boot and stopping dead. "Let me dance through the lot of you, let me think I'd scored the goal of the century, then fall about laughing. That the plan?"

Glancing at the players around her, Holly could see that plenty of sneering and smirking had already started. One crop-haired boy, his face creased by a wide, mocking grin, walked towards her.

"You sussed it early, but so what? Bottom line's the same. We don't want girls messing this up for us." He stopped a few metres in front of Holly, put his hands on his hips and puffed out his chest. His expression hardened. "Girls can't play," he sneered, almost spitting out his words. "Girls can't even kick."

Holly glanced down at the ball at her feet. She rolled it back, toe-flicked it up vertically, then tapped it up higher in front of her.

"Maybe you're right," she sighed, tapping the ball up higher still. "Maybe there is a difference between girls and boys." She looked set to tap the ball up again, but as it dropped, she suddenly volleyed it powerfully with her instep. The ball flew. She'd aimed at his lower stomach, but wasn't unhappy to see it thump into him just below that. He doubled over, gasping from the force of the blow. "Wouldn't be too sure we can't kick, though," Holly added, as she turned and walked away.

The youth crumpled to the floor. Mr Peterson, one of the coaches for the session, came running over. A tall, thin-faced American, abroad on a year-long coaching scholarship, he had been setting up cones for a training exercise on another part of the field. Holly piped up quickly, expecting trouble.

"You don't have to ban me from the course. I'm quitting," she said, heading off to collect her kitbag.

"Be a shame," the coach replied as they passed. "You sure got one heck of a shot on you. Hold up a minute, OK? I gotta check he's still in one piece . . ."

A little surprised by the American's comment, Holly

waited. She had time to unclip and shake loose her thick, shoulder-length dark hair, and to pull on a pair of tracksuit bottoms, before the coach trotted back over to her.

"I guess he'll live," Peterson confirmed with no hint of concern. "His name's Duncan Ramsey. Couple of other coaches warned me about him." Then Peterson smiled. "They said he would be a pain, so it's kinda neat to see him in some."

Holly shrugged. "He said girls couldn't kick. I put him straight."

"Ain't that the truth," nodded the coach. " I only caught the end of what was going on, but I figured it was something like that. I've heard told Ramsey and his pals didn't take too well to girls getting in on 'their game.'"

"So that's why I'm the only girl out here. If he's known for giving girls grief, that's probably why they're staying away. And I just thought there wasn't the interest."

"Yeah, at first I was mystified why so few girls had signed up," said Peterson. "Girls' soccer is huge back in the States. But then I heard about Ramsey, and his 'tactics'. See, none of the coaches have ever caught him directly intimidating anyone."

"So he's always got away with it," sighed Holly. "Makes sense, I suppose. He's the sort that always does."

Peterson stared thoughtfully at Holly for a moment, then added, "Well look, you're more than welcome to stick around, of course. Don't worry about Ramsey giving you any more trouble." Over on the field, Holly could see Ramsey getting to his feet. He gave Holly a vengeful glare from across the field. The fact that she was a girl no longer mattered – they were soccer enemies now. They both knew, if they ever played against each other again, he'd foul her as hard as he could, first chance he had. And while Holly didn't doubt Peterson's intentions, the way that she had been set up earlier showed that Ramsey wasn't alone in wanting her off the course. "I'll pass," was all she said.

"It's your call," replied the coach after a pause, and Holly sensed a trace of disappointment in his tone. It vanished in an instant, though, when he suddenly snapped his fingers. "Hey, hold up," he enthused, "there's some neighbours of mine – Della Ambrose and Denise, er, Lambert, I think. They meet up for what they call a kick session with a few other girl players, Wednesday nights on the Recreation Ground. They told me to send along any girls on the course who might want to join them. Interested?"

Holly's mood suddenly brightened. It hadn't been the best of mornings, but here at last was something to smile about. "Am I interested? Is Michael Owen fast?" she beamed, pulling her bag on to her shoulder. "I never say no to a good kick session. Just ask Ramsey!"

CHAPTER TWO

THE KICK-ABOUT

"**A**re you guys Della and Denise?" Holly called out, approaching the two girls.

She had spotted the pair knocking long passes to each other the moment she came through the Recreation Ground gates. Both had looked good – accurate with their passing, precise with their control – leading Holly to assume they were the girls Peterson had spoken about. She was in for a surprise, however.

"Uh-uh. I'm Nina. That's Cassy," replied the shorter of the two girls. "Hope they show up, though. We heard they play soccer here, and wanted to boost the numbers."

Before moving to the area, the Kerrigans had been told that there was a US military base fairly close by, so Holly didn't think it odd that once again she was talking, judging by Nina's accent, to an American. "That makes three of us. I'm Holly," she said. "Can I join you while we wait?"

Soon the three girls were in a triangle, spraying passes to each other. As she'd suspected, Nina and Cassy possessed good skills. Dark-haired Nina, of average height like Holly herself, did tend to power the ball straight, and just occasionally she overhit a pass. Cassy, though, tall with page-boy styled fair hair, was very accurate. Even when striking the ball with the outside of her foot, putting spin on it, she curled pass after pass at Holly, who barely had to move to trap them.

Gradually, in twos and threes, more players arrived. Sisters Bev and Chrissie Blake were the first of the regulars. Mel Sullivan, also a regular, brought along two other newcomers, Vickie Davenport and Rebecca Fuller. Antonella Sanchez and a large, round-faced girl called Jenny York, explained that Della had been held up looking after her younger brother because their mother was late home from work. But with enough players for two five-a-side teams, a game was quickly arranged.

Playing between makeshift goals of kitbags and sweat shirts, the five new girls took on the regulars. Holly soon realized the advantage was all with the regulars, not least because the strongly-built Jenny quickly showed she was quite useful in goal. She'd stopped two fierce drives from Nina and Holly herself before the regulars took the lead. Antonella, short and thin, almost fragile-looking, was a very tricky player with the ball at her feet, and she skipped past Vickie and Rebecca to set up Chrissie Blake for the goal.

"Come on, let's get stuck in!" encouraged Holly, swapping places with Cassy in goal. Moments later, Vickie did just that when Antonella set off on another jinking run. The new girl lunged in – an instant after her olive-skinned opponent had clipped the ball forward – to scythe Antonella's legs away from under her.

"Woah! Yellow card or what?" laughed Mel, a few steps back.

"Sorry! Sorry," pleaded the tackler. Her victim, grinning from ear to ear, simply held out a hand, and a relieved Vickie helped pull her upright again. Trotting back towards her own goal, Vickie made a cringing face at Holly. "Was a bit wild, wasn't it? Thing is, I've never played before. It's a lot different from how it looks on the TV."

"Forget it," soothed Holly. "Watch the ball, though. She's very skilful, but keep your eyes on the ball."

Mel took the freekick, rolling the ball square to Chrissie. Nina put in a challenge, the ball broke back to Mel and she thumped it first time. Holly, in truth not much of a goalkeeper, stretched and blocked the shot with her left leg, falling back as she did so. The ball bounced straight across to Bev. Not far out, with the goal at her mercy, she couldn't miss – yet almost did. Her side-foot shot was pushed too wide, only trickling home after hitting a kitbag post.

A gale of laughter came from behind them, followed by a deep-voiced shout of "You miss them, girl, you want shooting!" Back on her feet, Holly turned to see two more girls approaching. One, laughing again, and clearly the owner of the deep voice, was tall and broad. At the top of her muscular body, her round face beamed out from beneath long, beaded, dreadlocked hair.

The other girl was almost the opposite in every sense: short, thin, pale, blonde, even stern-faced and serious. "Late again. Della's fault, as usual," she snapped.

"Hey, good turn out, though," Della continued, ignoring Denise's comment, "We've enough here for a team, with someone left over to slice up the oranges for half-time!"

Introductions were made, Jenny made a few suggestions for reorganizing the two sides to include Della and Denise, and the girls got back to playing soccer.

Holly loved it. The game was lighthearted yet, despite the wide variation in players' standards, everyone was skilled enough to make it a contest. As the evening wore on, the others tired, and Holly's strength began to show. She was playing well, at the heart of every move put together by her side. It was exactly what she needed to take her mind off her father's problems.

With the scores in the twenties, and the light fading, they decided to call time. The girls sat in a rough circle, some pulling on sweatshirts, others just catching their breath. "You're good, girl. How many d'you score?" Della asked

Holly, between gulps from a mineral water bottle.

Holly shrugged. "Five or six, I suppose," she answered. She really didn't know.

"And then some!" put in Nina, "You had to be close to double-figures. How long you been playing?"

"Well, since I was pretty young. I had a lot of encouragement from my dad," Holly replied. "From my mother as well," she added urgently. "She's definitely, you know, helped me a lot."

"Cassy's mom got us started back in the States," said Nina. "Soccer's real huge back home. The next Women's World Cup is there too."

"That'd be something, huh? Playing in a competition like that," reflected Nina's friend Cassy. She hadn't spoken much at all, Holly realized, yet her words seemed to make everyone dream for a moment, bringing about a lull in the conversation.

Denise Lambert broke the silence. "Didn't catch your last names," she remarked, addressing the two American girls.

"Danson," replied Cassy, looking at her friend. Then she smirked and looked away.

Nina shifted uneasily, took in a deep breath, and said, "I'm Nina Zbigniewowski. Yeah, I know," she shrugged. "It's Polish."

"It's a mouthful is what it is," suggested Della, raising her eyebrows.

"You'd never get that on the back of your shirt if you played for a team in the Premiership," Jenny laughed.

"Er, well listen," put in Holly, looking to change the subject, "you said we had enough players here to form a team, Della, so . . . why don't we?"

There were lots of excited calls of "Yeah," and "Great idea." Della said, "Hey, I was only joking, but if enough of us are on for it, yeah, why don't we?"

Denise wasn't so sure. "But where would we play? Who would we play?"

"There's bound to be a local league around here," offered Holly. "Maybe we can get help from them. Maybe they'll know of any leagues for girls nearby."

"Or maybe some of the men's or boys' teams round about here have also got girls' teams," Mel suggested. "My brothers all play. We can start by asking them."

Vickie Davenport was shaking her head. "You should definitely do it, but you'll need more players. I mean, Becs and me, we'd never really kicked a ball before tonight. We'd be useless in a team."

"But you'll get better with practice," reassured Holly. "Put in a bit of work, and you'll be amazed how quickly you'll shape up. And we'd all improve if we were playing regular matches."

"We'd all have to!" scoffed Denise.

"We'll need a name," Nina said, and pretty soon everyone was throwing out suggestions. They decided fairly quickly that they wanted something which sounded strong, and not too "prissy". The Banshees and the Vixens were suggestions that received nods of approval, then someone came up with the Amazons. Della laughed and wasn't being very serious when she blurted out Amazon Villa, but most of the others loved it. Nina and Cassy did too, once it had been explained that there was a famous English team called Aston Villa.

It was settled and Amazon Villa GFC came into being, late on a balmy summer's evening.

CHAPTER THREE

EARLY DOORS

A week and two training sessions later, a team meeting was called. It took place in unusual surroundings. Cassy's mother was a driver at the military base, transporting personnel around the area in a single-decker bus which she occasionally drove home, and in exchange for Cassy's promise to wash dishes for a week, her mother let Amazon Villa hold the meeting on board.

Holly stood at the front, addressing the players occupying the seats. "I've done some checking with male leagues and the District FA," she announced. "And like they say, I've got some good news, and some bad news."

"Gotta be bad news first cos it travels faster," smiled Della.

Holly launched straight into it. "The nearest girls' league is based fifty miles away from here." She waited for the hubbub of groans to die down before going on. "Worse than that, we're already too late to join that league for the coming season."

Howls of protest erupted, and it was Denise Lambert's voice which cut through the din. "That's it, then. We're finished before we've even played a game!"

"Not quite," Holly corrected. "What we *can* do is arrange some practice matches against some of the teams from the nearest league. When you think about it, that's probably the best thing for us to do anyway. Jumping straight into a league without giving ourselves the chance to find our feet as a team is really asking for trouble." There were a few nods and murmurs of approval before Holly went on. "There's something else to consider. If we make them away matches, we won't have to scramble around trying to find somewhere to play. We can take our time to find a field where we really feel at home."

"So, like, is that the good news?" asked Nina, looking puzzled.

"It's way better than that," Holly continued, warming to the subject. "Remember you talked about the Women's World Cup? Well the District FA told me there's a special girls' tournament being organized for next Easter. The prize for the winners is only an all-expenses trip to the States to watch the final!"

For several seconds, the bus was a cacophony of shrieks and whoops. "We can enter that, can't we? Can't we?" begged Mel excitedly.

"Can we enter?" repeated Holly, pulling some folded paper from an envelope she'd brought with her. "Is Dennis Bergkamp a Dutchman?" she added, unfolding the competition's entry form and holding it aloft for everyone to see.

Led by Della, a prolonged bout of cheering gradually became a rousing chant of "Am-a-zons! Am-a-zons! Am-a-zons!" Eventually, Jenny York moved to the front of the bus to speak. "OK, OK, simmer down, you lot. Couple of things we've got to get straight. If we are going to do anything in that competition we'll have to roll our sleeves up. Loads of practice, training all through the winter, you name it. Next thing – Holly, you said it was fifty miles or so to those other teams. If we're playing away . . . "

Jenny let the sentence trail away, and Holly picked up the thread. "I know. Transport. Cassy," she said, turning to the quiet American. Holly spread her arms to indicate their surroundings. Creasing her face into a grimace, she asked, "Any chance?"

Cassy blew out her cheeks "Gee, I dunno," she sighed. "At this rate, I could end up washing dishes for a year!"

CHAPTER FOUR

A BAD START

Amazon Villa set off in bright sunshine to play their first ever match. The warm, pleasant September morning added to the general mood of optimism, for everything seemed to be going to plan. Cassy's mother, it turned out, pleased that her usually shy daughter had made so many new friends so quickly, was only too happy to drive the girls to the game. No one was late, and no one had forgotten her boots or shin-pads. The kit, a spare one borrowed from a team Mel's brother Roy played for, even looked like it would fit everyone. This was going to be a day to remember, everyone thought. And so it proved – though not for the reasons they all imagined!

Holly made sure she sat next to Vickie Davenport for the journey. Vickie, in the side at left full back, was starting her first ever eleven-aside soccer match. She was fine on all the basic rules, but Holly thought it would be useful to go over one or two of the specific ones with her. "OK, you're straight on the back-pass rule? If you, or anyone in our team, passes the ball to Jenny in goal, she can't use her hands to control it or pick it up, yes?"

"Got it," confirmed Vickie, "she has to kick it clear. That's all right – it's offside that I'm not sure of. I know there are times when a player can't be offside, like from a throw-in, or when she is in her own half for instance, but I get confused about which defender makes an attacker offside."

"Right. Offside is really all about where two players are at the instant when the ball is played forward. The two players are the attacker who is furthest forward and the second last opponent. Now, the goalkeeper is nearly always going to be the last opponent. That means the second last opponent is most likely going to be the last defender, the outfield player nearest her own goal-line." Holly paused, and Vickie's nod told her she was following the explanation. "OK, if the attacker is nearer the goal-line than the last defender when the ball is played forward, she is offside. But if she is level with, or further away from the goal-line than the last defender, the attacker is onside when the ball is played forward. That sometimes causes confusion – the key moment is when the pass is played forward, not when the attacker receives the ball."

Holly further explained that sometimes a referee might not whistle for offside if the attacker furthest forward was not interfering with play, or seeking to gain an advantage, when in an offside position.

"So if the ball goes into the net," Vickie wondered, "and if an attacker was in an offside position, but was maybe out at the side of the field, the ref might let the goal stand?"

"That's right. Causes a lot of arguments, though," smiled Holly. "The old saying is that if a player isn't interfering with play, what is she doing on the field!"

They spent most of the rest of the journey talking about formations. Vickie understood that the team was going to play with four defenders, four midfielders, and two attackers – or 4-4-2. It was the most common line-up in soccer, Holly told her, although she outlined some of the others. "Sometimes, teams switch formations during the game. They might push an extra player forward, to attack more. That's basically 4-3-3, although the third striker might play just behind the front two, rather than right up alongside them. Then again, there's 3-5-2, which has the full backs becoming wing backs. They have to be defenders one minute, then race forward up the wings to help the attack the next. They need to work very hard to make the system work." Vickie looked daunted. "Don't worry. We won't ask you to do that. At least," Holly joked, "not in your first game!"

Their opponents were a team called Dempsey's Diamonds. They played on one of a number of fields in a large park, and as the Villa bus arrived, several boys' games were in progress. Inside the bus the girls, who had been in high spirits on the journey, went very quiet.

A tall blonde lady, in her early forties Holly thought, approached the bus as the last few players climbed out of it. The woman went straight to Cassy's mother.

"Amazon Villa, I presume. Hello, I'm Sandra Dempsey," she said briskly, offering her hand. Cassy's mother looked phased for a moment, then quickly responded.

"She thinks your mother's our manager or something," Holly whispered to Cassy.

Once directed to the changing rooms, the Amazons were soon in their kit and out on the field. Their opponents, in an all-white strip with a large red diamond on the shirt, were circled around Sandra Dempsey. Last minute instructions, Holly decided. She hoped her chat to Vickie on the bus had been enough, and wondered if the whole team should have talked more about tactics.

The Amazons kicked off, and made a bad start. Bev Blake, playing up front with Nina, exchanged passes with her strike-partner, then rolled the ball to Antonella Sanchez wide on the right. Her first attempt at a run was stopped by a crisp tackle from a Diamonds player, who came away with the ball. She looked up, and sent a long pass arcing over Della and Chrissie Blake in the middle of the Villa defence. The centre forward for the Diamonds was very fast. Sprinting between Villa's centre backs, she galloped clear, and the ball fell right into her stride. She controlled it, advanced on Jenny in goal, fired a firm, low shot wide of the Amazon keeper, then whooped with delight when the ball nestled in the corner of the net.

With the next Diamonds attack, the bad start became a disastrous one. From the Amazon's second kick-off, the ball was pushed back to Cassy, alongside Holly in a central mid-field position. Several white-shirted players rushed at her. She panicked, and sliced her hurried pass straight to the opposition. The Diamonds swiftly switched the ball out to their right and Amazon Villa's left. Denise Lambert was bypassed easily. Vickie, looking determined, made a better attempt at a tackle, but mistimed it and up-ended the Diamonds winger. All the Amazon defenders froze, expecting the referee to give a free kick. The ball, though, had rolled to another Diamonds player. "Play on, play on!" shouted the referee, signalling that the advantage was with the home team. They quickly exploited it. The ball was passed forward into the Amazon penalty area, where the speedy number nine who'd scored the first goal raced in again. She thumped the ball hard, and although Jenny half-stopped it, the shot still had enough power to bounce up off her hands and into the net.

Holly shook her head in disbelief. Only minutes gone, and they were 2-0 down. She hadn't even touched the ball yet!

For the rest of the first half, Holly tried to rally her team-mates. She dropped deeper to help out the Amazon's troubled defence. She provided extra cover on the left, where Vickie and Denise had been struggling. And when the team did manage to work the ball into the opposition half – usually through good work by Antonella or Nina – Holly ran forward to give support.

After one such surge upfield, Holly even managed the only Villa shot of the first half. Put in the clear by Cassy, Antonella made good progress down the right wing. Holly, galloping through the centre, called for a lay-off inside when two defenders closed on her team-mate. Antonella obliged with a good pass. Controlling the ball with her first touch, Holly cracked it at the target with her second. It looked a goal all the way – until the Diamonds keeper dived full stretch to make a great save low to her right.

The keeper didn't wait for any praise. She rolled up to her feet, immediately throwing the ball accurately to a team-mate out wide. Villa's players, Holly included, were still reeling from the near-miss. They allowed their opponents to break quickly, down the left yet again, and carve out another chance for the dangerous centre forward. She put it away with a sharp finish for her hat-trick, and the Diamonds' third.

By half-time, it was 6-0. The shell-shocked Amazons gathered together during the break, and no one spoke at first. Della ended the gloomy silence, hoping to lift spirits at the same time. "We've got 'em worried," she said.

"This isn't funny Della!" snapped Nina. "We're being humiliated here. Don't any of you Brits care about it?"

Quite a few players protested at that. Tempers were fraying, and Holly had to shout to be heard above the raised voices. "Hold it! Hold it! Arguing amongst ourselves doesn't help. Now look, the game's gone. This isn't fantasy football – we're not going to bang in seven and win. But we can at least try and play better in the second half. Rebecca, you switch with Vickie like we agreed, and Bev, you'll have to drop deeper on the left to help Becs and Denise out because they've really hurt us down that side. Della and Chris, their number nine's given you the runaround, so how about if you stay tight on her Della, and Chris comes across behind you more as cover, instead of staying alongside. And everybody has got to work harder, got to give more. We're called Amazons. Let's play like Amazons."

Holly wasn't sure if her pep-talk had really worked, or whether the Diamonds had eased off, but for more than ten minutes at the start of the second half, the Amazons gave as good as they got. They created two good chances, although the keeper made another very good save to foil Nina with the first, and Bev Blake shot wide and weakly with the second.

But from the resulting goal-kick, taken by a tall, solidly-built Diamonds centre back who could thump the ball a huge distance, Holly's team were dealt a cruel blow. The kick reached the half-way line, where it was flicked on deeper into the Villa half. Giving chase was the fleet-footed centre forward. Della was at her shoulder, really straining to keep alongside, while Chrissie Blake was coming across diagonally. Suddenly, just inside the Villa penalty area, all three collided. They fell in an untidy heap, and an instant later there was a shrill blast on the whistle. "Penalty!" announced the referee, still some distance away from the incident.

Della and Chrissie were aghast. "But she fell and brought us down," protested Chrissie, who was then warned in no uncertain terms by the stern-looking ref not to show dissent by arguing back. The penalty was dispatched past Jenny York, and Chrissie, still murmuring to team-mates nearby that it wasn't fair, that it wasn't a penalty, lost all concentration. In the very next attack, she left another forward in too much space in the penalty area. When the ball found the striker, Chrissie couldn't recover, and Jenny was beaten an eighth time.

Once again, the Amazons had lost two quick goals, and once again, the side was rocked to its boots. Holly buzzed here and there trying to stem the tide of attacks, but the Diamonds were finding their way through to the Villa goal almost at will. Towards the end, when the team was really flagging, there was another flurry of goals. Even Holly herself was pleased to hear the final whistle. Amazon Villa were beaten 13-0.

Holly was one of the last to leave the changing room. Sandra Dempsey was waiting outside, seeing off some of her jubilant players. She hurried across to Holly.

"Bad luck," she said. "Goes like that, sometimes. Took some frightful hammerings myself when I was playing, till I found myself a decent team to play for." She paused, giving Holly the chance to reply. Holly said nothing. "You can play," the woman went on. "Shame about your team-mates. You play to win, but you won't win anything with them. Need to find yourself a decent team, you see. The Diamonds would be glad to have you."

Holly stopped walking. She stared ahead at her team-mates sitting sullenly on the bus. She chewed her bottom lip for a moment. Sandra Dempsey spoke again.

"You'd blossom, playing for us. You know you would."

"Thanks," replied Holly after a few moments. She was thinking hard. She was trying to work out what it was that made her dislike this woman so much. Perhaps it was the way she kept making assumptions.

"Thanks," Holly repeated, "but no thanks."

Sandra Dempsey raised an eyebrow. "Pity," she sighed, spinning on her heels to walk away. "Safe journey home."

The bus was quiet as Holly climbed on board. She passed row after row of dispirited faces, each one looking like a deflated soccer ball. She found a seat, sat down, and closed here eyes.

"13-0. Dad said there'd be days like this," she told herself.

THE FIRST GOAL

The thrashing from the Diamonds made the Amazon Villa girls realize just how much they all had to improve, both as players and as a team. To that end, everyone set about working much harder in training. Yet just as important, Holly thought, was the fact that nobody dropped out. Being prepared to come back and try again after taking such a battering showed character, something Holly's dad had always told her was vital to any successful player.

For the next one-and-a-half practice games the hard work brought improvements. The first of those games, a 7-1 defeat to a team called Elle United, was mostly a good performance. The scoreline would have looked far better except for three United goals in the last ten minutes, when many Villa players tired again. And the biggest plus, of course, was the goal.

Holly started the move, picking up a loose ball in the centre-circle before finding Antonella out wide. The tricky winger jinked her way past two players in a skilful run, then clipped the ball into the penalty box. Nina challenged for it with a defender. They both connected with the ball at the same time, causing it to spin up in the air. Nina put on the brakes, but the defender slipped and fell, leaving the Amazon forward clear. She controlled the spinning ball, took another touch to steady herself, then drilled a low shot across the United keeper into the far corner of the net.

Nina was mobbed by her team-mates. They charged forward to surround her from all parts of the field, and when Jenny York arrived from the Villa goal, adding her not inconsiderable weight to the celebration, the throng of players toppled over into a heap.

"You'd think they'd won the World Cup or something," scoffed one United defender.

More progress was evident in the first half of Villa's third practice game. At the break, they were 2-0 down, when, with better luck, it might have been 2-2. Before their opponents had scored, a shot from Bev Blake was cleared off the line. Then late in the half, a good run from Holly ended with a shot that cannoned back into play off a post.

"Forget the score, Amazons, that was a cracking performance," enthused Mel Sullivan as the team grouped together at the interval.

"Best we've played, by a mile," Nina added.

Holly was about to endorse that, while stressing the need to up their play even more if they could, when a male voice cut in from the sidelines. "Well done, Holly. It's looking good, girls, despite the score."

Several heads, including Holly's, turned in the direction of the speaker. "Dad!" she gasped in astonishment. Then she suddenly frowned, perplexed. "But . . . what about . . ."

Denise Lambert bluntly interrupted, recognizing the casually dressed, athletically built man on the sidelines. "Hang on! That's Mike Kerrigan. Signed for City last year, 'cept . . ." She let that sentence drift away as the penny dropped, her eyes shifting across to Holly. "Oh no wonder she's so flippin' good," she added sardonically, "her Dad's only a Premier League player!"

"Cool!" purred Della. "Could've told us, though, Hol."

"Why?" Holly protested defensively. "Doesn't make us a better team, does it?"

There was a short, awkward silence, broken by the referee signalling that she wanted to restart the game. The rest of the team trotted back to their positions while Holly walked slowly, glancing back at her father every few steps, as if to check he was still there.

She had a poor second half. Distracted, troubled even, it seemed to some, by her father's presence, her concentration had gone. Several other players lost form too, almost as if they felt nervous or embarrassed to be on the same field as someone with such a superior soccer pedigree. Inevitable consequences followed. The Amazons created very little in the second period, and as the game wore on, they began leaking goals. In the end, they lost badly, 8-0.

At the final whistle, Holly dashed away to the changing rooms. She didn't stop to change, but collected her belongings and departed with her father – all without uttering a word.

CHAPTER SIX

"I CAN'T PLAY ANY MORE"

"**W**hat happened to you lot in the second half?" Mike Kerrigan asked his daughter from behind the wheel of their car. They'd just turned out of the park, on to the main road.

Holly ignored the question, asking several of her own instead. "Should you be driving? What about your knee?"

Her dad sniffed. There was no point in putting off telling her. "It doesn't matter any more, sweetheart. The specialists in Geneva couldn't do anything for me. In the end, they said there wasn't enough cartilage left to work with. I'm through, Holly. I can't play any more."

Holly closed her eyes tight shut. She'd dreaded hearing such words from the moment she'd seen her father on the touch-line. He'd gone abroad a month ago in a desperate search for help with the injury he'd suffered in only his fourth game for City. In phone calls home, he'd told her he'd be away about eight weeks if the planned treatment was going to be successful. As she'd feared, his early return meant it hadn't been. Tears wet her cheeks. "Oh Dad . . ." she sobbed.

Mike pulled in to the curb, then pulled his daughter close to hug her. They sat in silence for a long time.

GETTING ON
WITH THE GAME

The next Amazon Villa training session took place about a week later. Holly, her enthusiasm dulled after recent events, arrived half-an-hour late – to discover that Bev and Chrissie Blake, and Rebecca, would not be arriving at all.

"They've had enough," Denise informed Holly gloomily. "Fed up taking a pasting every time they play. Can't say I blame them. I mean last week was awful, second half. Going backwards, we are, 'stead of improving."

Holly glanced around the group. Nina and Cassy, as ever, were kicking a ball about, but everyone else was slumped on the ground, in no hurry to start practising. Even Della looked down. She pulled a newspaper from her kitbag. It was several days old, and carried the story of how Mike Kerrigan's career was over.

"Read about your Dad, Hol. That's desperate, girl. We're all real sorry."

"Thanks, Della," Holly replied softly.

"What's going to happen?" asked Mel. "Are you going to move again, now your Dad's left City?"

Holly sighed. "It's possible, I suppose. We did only move

here because of Dad's transfer. Course by the time we'd bought the house and moved in, Dad was crocked."

"Well if you go," Denise put in bluntly, "that'll be the Amazons finished, won't it?"

Antonella Sanchez looked pessimistic. "I think maybe it's finished already," she said.

Several girls glanced at Holly, expecting her to put up an argument. Instead, she stayed with her head bowed, staring at the grass in front of her.

Vickie Davenport was irritated. "So is this what happens in girls' soccer, is it? Get beat a few times, then you pack it all in? I might be new to all this, but I didn't think we'd be that different from the blokes, because from what I've seen from my dad, my uncles, my Grandads, they never give up!"

While she spoke, Nina and Cassy rejoined the group. "Yeah, come on girls," Nina said, trying to lift the others. "Building a team's long-haul stuff. OK, it's been a little bumpy so far, but we gotta hang in there."

Holly knew Vickie and Nina were right. "Yes," she said to herself as much as anyone. "Time to get on with the game."

The girls warmed up, pinging passes to each other as they bounced on their toes. "What about Rebecca and the Blakes?" Mel wondered. "They might take a lot more convincing to come back. If they don't, we're going to need some new players."

Nina spoke up again. "I know what might bring them back. But . . ." She frowned, doubts already forming before she'd even given proper expression to her idea. "Don't know what you'll all think of this – 'specially you, Holly. And maybe it's impossible anyway. Maybe your dad's already got stuff lined up . . ."

Holly looked puzzled. "My dad? What's he got to do with this?"

"It's just – well, what this team really needs," Nina continued, "is a coach. Someone to train us properly, teach us tactics, improve our technique. And if that someone was a real player, a professional like your Dad . . ."

"Bev and Chrissie'd be back like a shot! Their family's City mad," cut in Mel.

"Becs would too! I'm sure of it," Vickie added.

Someone passed the ball to Holly, but she was standing still. It rolled into her legs, then stopped at her feet. She had never heard her dad talk of wanting to take up coaching when he finished playing. But the end of his career had come suddenly, far sooner than he'd expected. She knew he hadn't got a clue about what to do in the future.

"How about it, Hol?" asked Jenny, after a few moments. "Think he might consider it?"

There was a long pause before Holly replied. "Do I think he might consider it?" she repeated. "Does Mia Hamm train twice every day?"

Several of the girls exchanged curious glances. "Er, beats me," confessed Nina. "Does Mia Hamm train twice every day?"

"I've no idea," replied Holly.

CHAPTER EIGHT

HOLLY POPS THE QUESTION

"**N**o good asking me, love, is it?" said Holly's mother. Holly had decided to sound out her mother first on the subject of her dad but she wasn't getting a very positive response. "Right now I couldn't guess what he'll say about anything. Yesterday, I made him his usual cup of tea first thing, and he near-enough bit my head off. After all these years, suddenly he wants coffee in the mornings." Holly's mother paused. They were in the kitchen, preparing the evening meal. Laura Kerrigan stopped chopping vegetables and turned to her daughter, her expression taking on a look of concern. "He's very down, love. It's starting to really sink in with him that his career's over. Just be prepared for an answer you don't want to hear, if you do ask him."

"Ask him what?" said Mike Kerrigan, walking into the room.

Holly glanced at her mother. She took a deep breath, then went for it. "The Amazons need a coach, Dad. We're struggling a bit on our own. We need guidance, we need direction."

"Oh, and do I know someone who can help, you mean?

Well let's think . . ."

"No, Dad," corrected Holly. "We were wondering if you would coach us."

"Give over!" laughed her dad. His laughter faded when he read the expressions of his wife and daughter. "You're serious? Me coach your team? No. No way. That's ridiculous."

"Why? Because we're only girls or something?"

"No. Boys, girls – circus elephants, even – it makes no difference. Holly, I'm a player and . . ." He caught his breath, and corrected himself. "I *was* a player. Coaching is completely different. It's not for me."

"But it could be," Holly jumped in. "You've got all that training knowledge, all that playing knowledge – and for goodness' sake, you taught me to play!"

"I showed you how to kick a ball properly, and maybe a trick or two, that's all."

"Not true! You taught me everything I know . . . and now I love playing, as much as you . . . did." Holly was starting to get frustrated, and she couldn't stop herself from adding, "It's not as if you've got anything else to do right now is it – except sit around here and be miserable?"

"Hey young lady, that's enough! I've told you no, and that's it. Subject closed!" Letting out a deep breath, Mike Kerrigan thought that was that.

"No," said Laura suddenly and firmly. "The subject is not closed. Holly's got every right to tell you to pick yourself up. She's suggested something you could at least have a crack at, and I haven't heard one good reason yet why you won't try it."

Holly was a bit surprised by her mother's intervention. She usually stayed out of any discussions or arguments to do with soccer. When Holly was trying to keep it secret that her father was a professional, she'd let the others think that her mother was a big influence in her life, when really she had little interest in soccer. "Now it seems to me," Laura was continuing, "you've got something of an obligation to Holly. You got her started, told her what a wonderful game it was to play, and the rest of it. All against my wishes, you'll remember, but we'll let that pass. So it's down to you that she's reached a certain level, yet when she and her friends need help to go further, you throw out this 'coaching's not for me' line. How very convenient! Well you can wash your hands of it if you like, but no one's going to think you're much of a father or much of a person if you do."

Mike's mouth opened, seemingly to begin a reply, but then he closed it again. He looked away to a corner of the kitchen and let out a heavy sigh. Finally he gave his head a shake, as if to clear it. Very calmly he replied, "Don't know which is worse – the ear-bashings I used to get from the manager, or the ear-bashings I get from you." He walked to the kitchen door, watched every step of the way by Holly and her mother.

"I'll think about it," he called over his shoulder on leaving.

"That's what he says," Laura confided to Holly, "when he's going to say yes to something in a few days' time. I think you've got your coach."

Holly beamed at her mother. "You were . . . awesome!" she said with great admiration.

"Aye, well – you're not the only girl with a bit of mettle in this house," said Laura Kerrigan. She went back to chopping the vegetables. "Where d'you think you got yours from in the first place?"

THE FIRST TEAM

As Laura Kerrigan had predicted, Holly's father came along to coach the Amazons in their next training session. He was rather quiet and apprehensive at first, but when he saw how eager everyone was to learn, he warmed to the task. He kept things simple, setting the players to work on drills and exercises he'd done himself thousands of times down the years. To the girls, though, they were fresh, stimulating challenges which brought noticeable improvements to some even during that first session.

The three who'd missed training the last time were back in the fold. Everyone was so keen that Mike, drawn in by their enthusiasm, ended up doing forty minutes longer than planned.

"Well done everyone. Excellent session," he announced. "But keep at it. Work on your own with the ball when you have the chance, on touch, on control, on making the ball your friend. We'll go through plenty of close control and dribbling exercises next session."

"So," began Holly, throwing her kitbag on to the back seat of the car, "you'll definitely be taking our next training session then."

"Of course. Why not?" replied her dad.

"Oh, no reason," she said, smiling to herself.

Over the next few weeks, Mike helped a number of the

Amazon players improve substantially. Bev Blake became far more confident and relaxed with the ball at her feet. Cassy Danson, already an assured passer of the ball, was moving better off it. She was tackling better too, as was Mel Sullivan. But by far the biggest improvement was seen in Vickie Davenport. Every aspect of her game – control, passing, tackling, even heading – had been enhanced. She was unrecognizable from the slightly awkward girl who'd never played before when the Amazons first got together.

After one evening session, Mike told the others that he and Holly would be watching the big International match on the TV the following evening. In a throw-away remark, he said any girl interested in joining them would be welcome. He fully expected that most, if not all, would be busy. At seven-thirty on the night of the game, there was a knock at the door. Mike answered it, and found the entire Amazon Villa squad on his doorstep.

"Good grief. Mike, what's going on?" asked Laura, standing on the stairs and watching the girls file past her into the living room.

"Er, team-building session," offered Mike, off the top of his head.

His wife rolled her eyes to the ceiling. "Oh yes. And I suppose they'll all want feeding."

Mike clicked his fingers. "Pizzas! We'll have some delivered. I'll stump up for it."

"You certainly will," stressed Laura.

The evening was spent munching pizza, talking formations and tactics as the game unfolded, and toasting a convincing win by the national side.

Towards the end of the next training session, when the girls were playing six against six, a man wandered over to watch the game. Nobody noticed him, even when Mike stopped the play once or twice to explain about effective running off the ball and finding space to give the player in possession good passing options. It was only after Mike called time on the session, and the man approached, that Della spotted the observer.

"Hey, Mr Peterson," she called out. "What are you doing down here?" Holly recognized him then. He was the American coach from the Soccer Fun course, who had first told Holly about the girls' soccer games at the Recreation Ground, and who, she remembered, was a neighbour of Della's.

"Just wondered how you all were doing," Peterson replied, "and if you'd heard there was a girls' soccer tournament coming up at Easter."

"We know. We're in it," grinned Denise, who also lived close to the coach.

"Excellent," he enthused. "Got yourselves a trainer who knows his stuff, too." Holly introduced her father to Peterson, and while the girls pulled on warm tops and took drinks, the two men struck up a conversation. "Read about you in the paper. That was a real tough break with your injury," said Peterson.

"Yeah, no two ways about it. Even though I knew it was a bad one, it was still pretty devastating when they finally said 'Sorry Mike, career over'. To be honest, I'm still in a kind of limbo. Thought I had a few more years left, you see, so I hadn't got anything sorted about what to do after playing."

Peterson looked surprised. "But, you're coaching, aren't you? I mean, some of the things I saw you doing just now, that's textbook stuff, straight out of the coaching manuals." The American gave a little chuckle. "Stuff that took me years to learn!"

Mike was shaking his head. "I've never given coaching a second thought. I suppose I've picked things up from the coaches I've had, and from playing, but really, I'm only doing this for Holly."

"Well for sure, it wouldn't hurt to think about doing it for yourself, Mike," suggested Peterson. "A good coach is never going to be short of work, either here, or maybe in Europe. Or how about the States for that matter? The opportunities back home right now are huge."

Mike stayed silent, considering what he'd heard. "Say listen," Peterson added after a few moments, "there are some intensive courses around these days – Coaching For Coaches, I think they're called – which are kinda like fast-track qualification schemes for people already in the game. Something like that could be right up your street."

"Certainly worth thinking about," Mike reflected. "Thanks."

The girls had packed up. Holly and her Dad said their goodbyes and headed for the car. "This Easter tournament you're in – what's the prize again?" Mike asked.

"The prize for the winning side," Holly began, remembering word for word what was written on the leaflet, "is an all-expenses-paid trip to the United States, to watch key games, including the final, of the 1999 FIFA Women's World Cup."

"Interesting, said Mike, nodding to himself. "You know, if you do pull it off and win, maybe we should combine it with a holiday for your mother and me, too. Make it a real family trip."

"Sounds great to me," smiled Holly.

"And you never know," Mike shrugged, "a competition at that level might even get your mother interested in soccer."

They both turned to look at each other, then shook their heads. "Nah!" they said together. The tournament was just a month away. Holly had two further practice matches to arrange. Mike suggested that to give the team a feel for tournament conditions, when a number of games had to be played in a short space of time, the two practice matches should take place over one weekend. Holly had no trouble in arranging exactly that.

Three days before the games, Mike sat down with Holly, Nina and Della to discuss a few things.

"Now then, I've singled out you three for a couple of reasons. First, correct me if I'm wrong, but you're more or less the senior players in the team. You're basically the leaders – most of the other girls look up to at least one of you. Second, you each play in a different area of the field; Della at the back, Holly in midfield, Nina up front. That's important. It gives us a key player, a captain if you like, in each part of the team, and right through its centre. You three are the backbone of the team. And every successful side there's ever been was built around a good spine." Mike paused, glancing from girl to girl to make sure they were still with him.

Della grinned. "Keep going. Got a biology test in the morning – this is like revision!"

"All right," smiled Mike. "So you're each a captain in your part of the field, but teams only have one official captain."

"Which is Holly," Nina remarked, wondering where this was going. "She's our best player."

"That's not really for me to say," put in Holly. "But there are better reasons to choose a captain than that."

"Exactly," added Mike. "Now, there are different ideas about this, but I've always liked my captains to play in defence. For one thing, they are more or less facing the play, looking at everyone on the field, all the time. They can see everything, like if there are gaps somewhere, if a team-mate isn't doing her job, whatever. Midfielders and strikers, who have to keep looking in different directions – forwards sometimes, backwards sometimes, even sideways sometimes – can miss things."

"Hold on a second," frowned Della. She looked a little worried. "You suggesting what I think you're suggesting?"

"You're perfect for it, Della." enthused Holly. "Right temperament. Right position on the field. Even right voice – you could make yourself heard at Wembley when a goal's just

42

been scored! I'm not much of a captain anyway, I get too wrapped up in the play."

Nina was nodding her head. "Makes sense to me." She grinned when she added, "Besides who's going to argue with you? You're bigger than everyone else!"

"You for one, girl, when I open my big mouth and make some stupid joke – like at half-time in our first game."

"Being funny is a great way to win your team-mates over, Della," said Mike. "All you really need to do is work out when to crack a joke, and when to crack the whip. Do that, and you'll be a great captain, believe me."

With everyone showing such faith in her, Della bowed to the inevitable and agreed to be the new Amazon Villa captain. Mike then moved on to his thoughts about positional changes. "OK, now I've been watching Cassy closely. She's been playing in midfield because of her passing, but she's also moving better and tackling better these days. I think she'd make a great centre back, alongside you Della."

"Yeah? Maybe so," the new captain thought out loud. "She's tall enough to deal with any high balls knocked into the box, no problem."

"She can still make good use of the ball from defence, too," Holly suggested. "She just needs to hit longer passes, from deeper. You know her better, Nina. Can she play at the back?" The American pondered for a moment. "I don't think she's ever played there in her life. But, that doesn't mean she couldn't do it. Maybe it's worth a try. And we've got to do something about the defence, the number of goals we've conceded."

"Well following on from that, Holly told me you've been stretched down the left a few times," said Mike. "We could strengthen that side with Chrissie Blake, now we're playing Cassy at the back. Full back, or midfield, though?"

"Way she's been coming on, maybe Vickie's a bit wasted at left back," answered Della.

Holly nodded vigorously. "Definitely. We should give her a shot at midfield, in Cassy's old position."

"If we do that," replied Nina, sliding the fingers of her left hand back along the table top, "pull Denise back, and stick Chrissie in front of her. She's more mobile than Denise, and won't get bypassed so easily."

Mike pulled all those suggestions together, and wrote out the following line-up, in a 4-4-2 formation.

Jenny York

Mel Sullivan   Della Ambrose   Cassy Danson   Denise Lambert

Antonella S.   Holly Kerrigan   Vickie Davenport   Chrissie B.

Nina Z.   Bev B.

Sub: Rebecca Fuller

There were nods of approval from the three girls as they studied it.

"Don't know about you two, but I can't wait to play again," said Nina. "Feels just like we're starting over."

A TASTE OF GLORY

Tilston All-Stars were the opponents for the first match that weekend. They played at a neat, tree-lined ground which had a small stand for spectators on one side of the field. Quite a few of the spaces in the stand were occupied; the All-Stars were clearly a well-supported team.

"Focus only on the field. Don't worry about those people watching. And take no notice of anything they say," Mike advised. The players were gathered around him on the field, listening to a last-minute pep-talk. He'd planned to say something else, but had spotted looks of apprehension on the faces of one or two of the players, because they'd never played in front of anything resembling a crowd before. "Focus only on the field," he repeated. It was something he'd been told when he was a young player, something that had helped him considerably. "Concentrate on the game, and everyone watching just disappears, believe me. Now you've worked really hard in training. You're all better than the last time you played. So be positive. Believe in yourselves and believe you can win – because you can."

Amazon Villa kicked off, and Mike knew at once his words had worked. Any apprehension that had existed was now replaced by looks of determination. Right from the start, they took the game straight to the All-Stars.

Vickie and Holly worked the ball out wide to Antonella Sanchez, who set off on a dribble. Her mazy run took her past two defenders before she fired a cross-field pass for Bev Blake. She controlled the ball with her first touch, then prodded it forward for Nina who was making a diagonal run ahead of her. From just outside the penalty area, the American striker crashed the ball goalwards first time. Her fierce shot beat the goalkeeper, only to thump hard against the crossbar. The ball bounced down in the penalty area, where a defender hacked it away before Nina, following up, could reach it.

For the next twenty minutes the Amazons were in complete control of the game. They created chance after chance, and shots rained down on the All-Stars' goal. Time and again, however, the shots were saved, blocked, or flew narrowly wide. Watching from the sidelines, in front of the stand of spectators who were subdued by the way their team was being made to struggle, Mike was delighted with Villa's performance. Yet as he called encouragement from the touch-line, a flickering of doubt began to creep across his mind. He'd played in similar games many times before, when one side was so dominant, but for one reason or another, couldn't score. Often in such circumstances, the opposition wriggled off the hook, and scored themselves.

Another promising Villa attack ended with a desperate clearance from the All-Stars. The ball was thumped high and long upfield, in the general direction of their lone striker. She willingly gave chase, but Denise and Cassy were both in better positions to deal with the ball. Unfortunately, they both left it for the other. The ball bounced between them, while the striker gained ground, sensing hesitation. Cassy at last took charge and went to hook it clear. Her boot connected cleanly with the ball, but her clearance hit the onrushing striker, ricocheted first off her, then off Denise, before bouncing back into the path of the All-Star. Roared on by those in the stand, the All-Star player raced clear of both Amazon defenders, towards Jenny York in goal. She came forward as she knew she must, "narrowing the angle" – or giving the striker as little of the goal to shoot at as possible – as all the textbooks demanded. The All-Star striker slowed to steady herself, and Cassy had almost caught her again when she clipped a deadly accurate chip shot. The ball rose swiftly, cleared Jenny and her upstretched arms, then started to drop, finally bouncing under the crossbar and into the net.

The supporters in the stand shouted loudly, acclaiming the goal. The Amazons looked stunned. Even Holly looked perplexed – they'd had countless efforts at goal but had nothing to show for it, while the All-Stars had scored with their one and only chance.

Confidence rocked, Amazon Villa lost their way. With plenty of noise from their supporters, the All-Stars took control and scored again minutes later. With Vickie snapping at her heels, trying to make a well-timed challenge, an opponent from midfield carried the ball towards Jenny York's penalty area. She let fly with a powerful shot that Jenny did well to stop, but couldn't hold. The rebound went straight to another All-Stars player, who fired the ball hard first time past the helpless Villa goalkeeper.

If the Amazons were stunned by the first goal, the second angered them. "I don't believe this!" fumed Holly.

"Yeah, come on, Amazons!" Della's voice boomed out. "No way have they been two goals better than us!"

The captain's words seemed to strike a chord with the other players. Feeling the scoreline was an injustice, everyone tried that bit harder to correct it. By half-time, though, Amazon Villa were still trailing 2-0.

"It's like the last game all over again!" complained Denise when the players grouped together. "Two down when we shouldn't be."

"No!" snapped Della. "This is different. We're gonna

make it different, second half." She said it with such conviction that several others shouted out their agreement.

"I'm certain of it," added Mike. He was speaking quietly but firmly, with a lot of authority, glancing from player to player in turn and holding their gaze for a few moments as he did so, as if to impress his thoughts upon them. "Maybe some of you have heard people on TV saying soccer can be a cruel game. Now you know what they mean. Sometimes you don't get what you deserve from a game, and this scoreline is a travesty. But you can put it right in the second half. I get the feeling you're all made of sterner stuff than to want to throw in the towel after a couple of bad breaks. Just play like you did in the first half – aside from those dodgy five minutes – and that scoreline must change."

The second period began much like the first, with Villa pressing and the All-Stars defending. Yet as before, the visitors couldn't find the net. And all the time, the danger was that the All-Stars would break away, score a third and finish off the Amazons for good.

Mike thought exactly that was going to happen after a Villa corner. Holly took it, aiming for Della's head. She'd come up from the back to add her height to the attack, and as the ball came over she flung herself at the cross. She missed it by a whisker, the ball was headed clear, and suddenly, with Della out of position, the All-Stars were counter-attacking. "Oh no," Mike whispered under his breath. The ball was swiftly knocked upfield for the scorer of the first goal to chase. Only Cassy was back, but in her first ever game in defence, she read the situation like a veteran.

As the striker took possession and tried to go outside her, the American turned, matched her opponent stride for stride, then stretched out her leg to hook a foot around the ball and win possession back for Villa. Not content with that, striding back towards the half-way line with the ball, she looked up, saw Della still in attack after the corner, and struck a glorious long pass towards her. Despite two defenders jumping with her, Della rose highest and headed Cassy's pass down into space. Holly, sprinting forward, saw the chance. She angled her run to meet the ball on its second bounce, connecting with her right boot. From some way outside the penalty area the ball screamed into the back of the net.

Team-mates rushed to acclaim her wonderful goal, but Holly kept the celebrating to a minimum. "We're still losing," she reminded the others. "Concentrate! We've still got a lot more to do."

On the touch-line, though, in front of the muted stand of All-Stars supporters, Mike was leaping up and down, punching the air excitedly. His joy as a coach was doubled by his joy as a dad. Someone in the stand who recognized him was surprised.

"Never saw him do his nut like that when he scored himself," the supporter muttered.

The Amazons pressed forward again, looking for the equalizer. The All-Stars defended stubbornly. The minutes ticked by. With scarcely any time left at all the All-Stars suddenly broke away again. They look destined to wrap up the win when the ball came through to a full back, overlapping on the left. She shot fiercely, but Jenny York stretched to pull off a fantastic one-handed save, and Mel Sullivan hammered the ball away. She was just looking to clear the danger, yet the ball arrowed to Antonella, in an ocean of space out on the right.

She sped forward, spotted an angled run from Bev Blake, and drilled the ball forward into the penalty box for her. Two defenders were tracking Bev, who looked set to shoot as the ball came to her. Instead, she touched it back and inside, fooling both defenders. Nina was following up and she pounced on Bev's lay-off. She could have thumped it first time at the goal, but took the ball in her stride with a sure touch. The keeper, expecting the early shot, dropped to one side trying to check her dive, leaving the rest of the goal open for Nina. As calm as if she were in training, she stroked the ball into the bottom corner of the net.

It proved the last meaningful kick of the match, the referee whistling for full-time shortly after. The Amazons had a draw, but having battled so hard, and having come back from two goals down, it felt like a win. Coming off the field, the players hugged and embraced each other. Applause echoed down from the stand of supporters, as much for the Amazons as the All-Stars. Mike Kerrigan was clapping enthusiastically too, a broad grin creasing his features.

"Well played, you lot. I'm proud of you. Just don't take as long getting changed as you did getting level in the game!"

While Mike waited outside the dressing room, a crop-haired boy wandered past. He stopped and turned to stare, his curiosity getting the better of him.

"You Mike Kerrigan? Used to play for City?" Mike nodded. The boy, who had a rolled-up soccer magazine with him, asked, "Any chance of an autograph?"

"Sure," replied Mike, "but maybe you should be asking my players for theirs. Did you see the game?"

"Nah. My mate did," said the boy. He began unrolling his magazine. "Said it was good stuff, but . . ." Instead of finishing his sentence he just pulled a face.

"Well, for what it's worth, your mate was right," suggested Mike, preparing to write on the magazine. "Who should I make this out to?"

"To Duncan Ramsey – dinosaur brain!" called out Holly. Emerging from the dressing room, she had recognized the boy from the Soccer Fun coaching course immediately. "He's not what you'd call a big fan of girls' soccer, Dad."

"You two know each other then?" enquired her father. "Sort of," put in Ramsey. His eyes darted from Mike to Holly several times. "My mate said he saw you in the game. I never realized your Dad . . ." Holly fixed him with a cold stare.

"Well anyway, my mate told me you scored. A beauty, he reckoned." Mike handed the magazine back. "So, er, maybe I was wrong, you know. Maybe . . . some girls can kick after all. Cheers for this." He waved the magazine, backed away a few steps, then disappeared around a corner.

"What was that all about?" Mike wondered.

"I think," reflected Holly, "that he's just begun to realize how big a game soccer really is . . ."

The Amazons arrived for the second match that weekend in buoyant, confident mood. They got into their stride early in the game, and took a deserved lead following yet another confident finish from Nina. Antonella Sanchez added to the lead before half-time, putting the Amazons firmly in control. The opposition tried to rally after the break, but Mel, Della, Cassy and Denise were showing signs of becoming a strong back-line. Together they dealt with most attacks, leaving Jenny York with scarcely a save to make.

Bev Blake got on the scoresheet to stretch the lead before coming off to give substitute Rebecca Fuller a run out. She busied herself in all parts of the field, showing what a useful squad member she was. Late in the game, she combined well with Nina to set up her friend Vickie Davenport for another goal.

Comfortable 4-0 winners at the end, the score did not flatter the Amazons.

"Can you believe it, Becs?" Vickie asked her friend on the journey home. "A few months ago we'd never played this game. Look at us now . . ."

"I know. And you especially," answered Rebecca. "So what's it feel like when you score a goal?"

Nina, in the seat in front, turned around quickly. "It's way cool, is what it's like. Way cool!"

"Yeah. Way cool," Vickie added, badly mimicking Nina's American accent, and all three burst out laughing.

CHAPTER ELEVEN

DEALING WITH A BAD BREAK

Ten days before the Easter tournament was due to begin, Holly and her dad were about to set off for an Amazons training session when the phone rang. Mike answered, and Holly killed time kicking a ball on the driveway. After several minutes, and keen to get going, Holly returned inside to hurry her father up. "It has to be that weekend? When will the next one be?" she heard him saying. "Oh. I see . . ." he continued in a disappointed tone. He sighed heavily, his shoulders sagged. "Well, yes, I want to do it, but . . . OK then yes, count me in . . . Yes certain . . . Thanks. I'm sure it will be too. See you then, Gerry. Bye."

He replaced the receiver and stared at it for several seconds.

"Dad," Holly called out, snapping him out of his thoughts. "Not a problem, is there?"

His hesitation in replying told her something was up. Eventually he said, "Sort of, but it can wait. Hey look at the time – we'd better get moving."

Nothing more was said on the subject on the journey to the Recreation Ground, or during training. Holly sensed he was not completely at ease, though, and she frowned with concern when he ended the session ten minutes early and called the girls together.

Fresh from a first ever win – "And a first clean sheet," Jenny kept stressing – everyone else had been bubbling. "Stopping early – you going soft on us, boss?" laughed Della.

Mike's smile was thin and forced. "Not quite," he managed to reply, before he began in earnest. "Girls, there's no easy way to put this. Cutting straight to it, I can't be with you for the Easter tournament." There were expressions of confusion and bewilderment, and one or two groans of protest. Several pairs of eyes darted in Holly's direction. The look of wounded puzzlement on her face told everyone she knew nothing of this. "I'm sorry, really sorry," Mike went on. "When I packed in playing, I hadn't a clue what I was doing. Coaching definitely wasn't on the agenda. Then I started helping you, and I've had such a buzz from it. Seeing you improve, seeing you develop as players. Seeing it all coming together on the field last weekend. You've opened my eyes, really, and I want to take a shot at coaching full time, especially after some of the things your mate Mr Peterson said. "To do that, I've got to complete some courses, earn the proper badges and qualifications. Peterson mentioned some scheme which is for ex-players. Trouble is, I've just found out from the guy running it that the next one is over the Easter Weekend – and he doesn't know when, or even if, there'll be another one. It's as good a chance as I'll ever get to kick-start a coaching career. And you know what you've got to do with chances in soccer . . ."

Mike's words hung in the air until Nina broke the silence. "You gotta take 'em," she said in a quiet, resigned voice.

"Guess we're back on our own again, girls," muttered Denise Lambert bitterly.

Della sprang to her feet. "Yep, that's the way it is!" she declared brightly. "And you know what? Maybe it's right it's worked out this way. Mike's been brilliant for us, but it was us girls who started this team, and it's us girls who it's really all about."

"Still can't help thinking it's a bad break, though," put in Jenny York.

"So what? Soccer's full of them. It's how you deal with them that matters," Della insisted. "And any girl who feels let down has got her head mixed up. All we should feel is grateful. We've been lucky, and I mean way lucky, that Mike's helped us as much as he has. So what's it to be, girls? Are we wussies, or are we Amazons?"

"Go Amazons!" shouted the usually placid Cassy. "And thanks for spotting I could play centre back, Mike." Quite a few others realized they had much to thank Holly's father for, and they began to express their appreciation. In the end, a burst of applause began spontaneously, signalling the end of the meeting. The only girl not to join in the clapping was Holly.

"You know, team coach or not, I would be there for the tournament if I could," Mike told Holly on the journey home. Holly stared ahead out of the windscreen, and said nothing. Driving along, her father glanced across to her several times. His hands tightened on the steering wheel. "Actually," he reflected, braking and pulling over to the kerb, "maybe you're right."

With the car stationary, he fished out a mobile phone from his tracksuit pocket.

"What are you doing?" asked Holly.

"Getting in touch with Gerry. Letting him know I can't make the course after all."

Holly let her eyes close for a few seconds. "Wait!" she called out suddenly. "You don't . . . you don't have to do that, Dad."

"Holly . . ."

"I know. I know I'm changing my mind like some teams change their kits. It's just . . . when you said you couldn't make the tournament, it really hurt. I wanted you there to coach the team, but also I wanted you there just because you're my dad. You were telling the team how sorry you were, but you never said anything to me." Mike chewed the inside of one lip, and felt guilty. "And just now, what you said when we were driving. It didn't really sound like you meant it. It was only when you started phoning that I believed it, that watching me play soccer meant anything to you."

"It means a great deal to me, love." Mike replied, "And you're right, I should have told you that before now. I should have told you what a cracking player you are becoming, and how good that makes me feel. I should have told you how proud of you I am." He reached an arm across her shoulders. Holly glanced over to him. Her face broke into a warm smile. "Oh, and when you scored that goal at the weekend," Mike grinned. "I thought I was going to explode or something!"

"Yes. Saw you out of the corner of my eye," said Holly, a note of mock rebuke in her voice. "Maybe it's just as well you can't make the tournament. You could get seriously embarrassing if I scored the winner!"

CHAPTER TWELVE

ON THE BRINK

The first stage of the 16-team tournament was on Easter Saturday. Amazon Villa were drawn in one of four groups, along with Sloneton Rangers, Miss Kickers, and a team they'd played before, Elle United. Each side was to play each other once, with the winners of each group progressing to the second stage, to be played on Easter Monday. The second stage comprised two semi-finals, with the winners of those to face each other in the final. The prize for the overall champions, of course, was the wonderful trip to the Women's World Cup Finals in the USA.

As usual, Cassy's mother drove the girls to the sports complex where the tournament was taking place. Quite a few other parents and supporters made the trip too, so the bus was full. On board, the atmosphere was charged with nervous expectation. Mel Sullivan's brother Roy was among the supporters, though when he joked he'd only come along to support his team's old kit, he was jeered noisily.

The complex itself covered a vast area. Behind two large indoor sports halls were a hockey field, a rugby field, and three soccer fields. A fourth was situated inside a stadium adjacent to the sports halls. The semi-finals and final would be played in the stadium, as well as all the games between the teams in Group A. This included, Holly noticed when she checked the roster and timetable, Dempsey's Diamonds. The Amazons had been drawn in Group C, so were set to play their games on one of the outside fields.

The girls made their way into the busy changing room area. Holly, who had butterflies in her stomach herself, could see that a number of her team-mates were looking tense. Up until now, they had technically only ever played practice games; the group games to come were going to be the team's first truly competitive matches.

Holly put her bag down on a bench and unzipped it. She reached inside for her kit, but her hand found something flat and smooth. She pulled it out. It was a large photo of joyous, celebrating women soccer players clustered around an elegant gold trophy. They all had medals around their necks. "Hey," said Nina, peering over Holly's shoulder, "that's the Women's World Cup. That's the USA team, when they won the first tournament, back in 1991." Holly checked the reverse side of the photo, where she found a brief message. It read, "A photographer friend tracked this down. Thought it might inspire – they're winners, just like you." Holly recognized her dad's handwriting, and smiled

The first game was against Miss Kickers. Holly's butter-flies faded almost with the blast of the ref's whistle to start the game, but even after several minutes, some of her team-mates were still making nervous errors. Antonella Sanchez, usually one of Villa's brightest attackers, was particularly off her game. She couldn't get going at all, giving the ball away on countless occasions. With her confidence evaporating, she stopped wanting the ball, stopped moving into space for passes. "Hiding," Holly's dad had called it. It meant the Amazons struggled to create any real openings. Fortunately, their opponents were just as tense and weren't playing any better themselves. The rather scrappy first half finished goalless.

Della, Holly and Nina took it in turns to gee up their

team-mates during the interval. They kept everything positive, stressing the game was there to be won if they just relaxed and got back to something like the form shown in their last two practice games. The message got across to all but Antonella. While the team started to function better, she continued to struggle.

Nevertheless, the breakthrough came five minutes into the second half. Holly and the Blake sisters combined well on the left, passing the ball in neat triangles to carve open the Kickers defence. Collecting a pass from Holly, Bev Blake turned sharply and, shifting the focus of the attack, threaded the ball through to Nina in the penalty box. She stretched out a leg to guide a low shot past the keeper's dive for the opening goal.

The Amazons pressed home the advantage with their very next attack. Vickie Davenport won possession with a sharp tackle in midfield, then raced forward with the ball. She looked for Bev on the edge of the penalty area with a pass. A defender challenged, the ball broke loose, and Holly, eating up the ground, pounced on it. She hit it first time, her unstoppable shot finding the top corner of the net.

Two goals to the good, the Amazons took complete control. Untroubled by the struggling, fading Kickers, two further strikes from Nina and Bev sealed a 4-0 win. The only concern was Antonella. Even after the team had built a comfortable lead, she couldn't find her form. At the final whistle, when the others noisily congratulated each other on winning three points and began a chant of "Am-a-zons! Am-a-zons!" she stayed silent.

Once the early excitement of the win had died down, Holly and Nina headed off to the changing rooms and toilets. Other group games had just finished, so the area was quite busy. While they waited at a water tap, Nina felt a hand on her arm.

"Nina, ain't it? Sorry, don't recall your last name – 'cept

that it was something long!"

Nina turned, then her face brightened with recognition. "Annie! Annie Devlin! What in the world . . . you playing here today?"

"Sure. For a bunch of American Service kids, Maybury Mavericks. You too?"

"Yeah. Amazon Villa, group C. Oh, this is my team-mate, Holly Kerrigan."

The tall, slender American, her long blonde hair tied back in a pony-tail, offered her hand to Holly. "Hi. How's it goin'?"

"Fine, how are you?"

"To be honest, dying for the can! I gotta go – see you guys later, huh?"

The Villa players wandered back to their group area.

"Know her from home," Nina volunteered. "We played up front together for the same junior side one season. She's a player, all right. Real sharp, and a great finisher."

"Did she say her team were all players from the States?" asked Holly.

"Yeah well there's another, much bigger US airbase at Maybury. Team's probably made up of girls from there."

"Likely to be any good?"

"If they're of Annie's standard," stressed Nina, "you bet they'll be good!"

Holly and Nina joined Della to watch the second game in their group, between Elle United and Sloneton Rangers. A discussion started about the make-up of the team for Villa's next match. It had always been the plan to rest some-one and bring in Rebecca Fuller for the second game. The question was who. Before it could be addressed, though, Chrissie Blake, limping slightly, hobbled up to join them.

"Took a bit of a knock towards the end out there. Nothing serious, but maybe I should sit out of the next one, give Becs a game."

Della turned to Holly and winked. "This team selection is easy." Holly grinned, but she did wonder, if Chrissie hadn't said anything, whether it would have been Antonella who they'd have left out.

With so many matches to be completed on the day, and because teams needed a sufficient rest period between games, everyone was playing shortened matches of twenty minutes each way. This counted against Elle United in the match Holly was watching. The team that had once put seven past the Amazons started cautiously. It was the second half before they really got into their stride. By then, however, the well-organized opposition were defending keenly too. Had the game been of normal length, Holly suspected United would have found the net and run out winners. The referee's watch foiled them, though, leaving the teams to share a point each. At 0-0 it was the best result the Amazons could have wished for.

They took on the Rangers in their next game, and avoided the problems Elle United had suffered by getting off to a flying start. In the first Villa attack, a shot from Nina was blocked, but the ball ran loose to Bev Blake. Her shot squeezed between keeper and post, giving Villa the lead. They never looked back. Rangers, solid defensively as they'd shown against Elle United, had little to offer going forward. When Nina doubled the lead midway through the second half, that was that. There was just one disappointment – Antonella had another poor game.

"Two games, six points. Excellent!" enthused Nina, exchanging high-fives with her team-mates as they gathered at the side of the field. "Six goals for, none conceded," she went on. "Are we hot or what?"

While the girls continued congratulating each other, Holly saw Antonella peel away towards her father, who had travelled with the team on the bus. Neither of them looked happy. They shared cross words and angry gestures before the winger came back to find her kitbag, her face like thunder. "I never play well when he's watching. Never, never!" Holly heard Antonella complain to herself. She grabbed her belongings and hurried away.

Holly joined Della again to watch the next game in the group, Elle United against Miss Kickers. United were far stronger and led 3-0 at the break. "They've got this in the bag," remarked Della.

Holly agreed. "They'll have four points, we've got six. Our match against them decides everything. Winners take all."

Della glanced across at her team-mate. "Draw's good enough for us. Means we'll finish top of the group, two points clear."

"We can't play for a draw. That's asking for trouble."

"Suppose so. Really rock 'em if we grabbed another early goal, wouldn't it?"

"Definitely!" Holly stressed. "We should go for it, you know, right from kick-off. They probably won't be expecting that."

A broad grin broke out across Della's face. "Hey listen to us, Hol. Few months back they thrashed us 7-1. And here we are, planning to dump them out the competition! I'm telling you, girl, this team's come a long way . . ."

"It's going further too, as long as we play this right," smiled Holly.

Nina joined them, and agreed that the Amazons should attack hard from the start. "OK, if those are the tactics, what about the team?" asked the striker. "If Chrissie Blake comes back in, who goes out?"

The three fell silent for a moment. "All right, I'll say it," began Della, suspecting they were all thinking the same thing. "On form, it has to be Antonella. She's really struggled so far."

"For sure. But, the trouble is," Nina reflected, "she's such a dangerous player at her best. Can we afford to leave her out?"

"Can we afford to leave her in if she's not contributing?" countered Holly. The other two shook their heads, settling the matter.

It meant the only thing left to decide was how to break it to Antonella. Eventually Della said it had to be the captain's job.

"Not looking forward to it, though," she sighed. She gave Holly a sideways look as she got to her feet. "What was I saying about team selection being easy?"

Later, Della told Holly she hadn't had to say much. Antonella was sitting apart from the others, looking miserable. Her arms were wrapped around her legs which were drawn up to her chest. Her chin was resting on her knees. She knew what was happening when the captain approached. "You dropping me?" she asked.

"Leaving you out," Della corrected, seeking to soften the blow.

Antonella shrugged and pulled a face. "It's fair," was all she said before returning to her own brooding thoughts.

With Chrissie Blake back in her favoured position of left midfield, Rebecca Fuller switched flanks to fill Antonella's place on the right. The deciding game of the group began with the Amazons, as planned, attacking from the off. Their first move ended with a crisp shot from Nina which was goal-bound until a United defender stuck out a leg and deflected the ball wide for a corner. Della, up from the back, leapt well to meet the corner kick with a firm header. The ball flew from her forehead, beat the goalkeeper's flailing arms, but slapped hard against the crossbar, rebounding for a United player to hack it clear.

Carrying the game to their opponents, Villa made further chances. Bev Blake put one shot just wide, Nina and Holly had good efforts well saved, and Rebecca shot tamely, straight at the keeper, when in a great position. But a breakthrough goal never came, and towards half-time, when

United came more into the game, Jenny York in Villa's goal had to make two sharp saves. Despite the abundance of chances the game was scoreless at the interval.

"Come on, Amazons," exhorted Holly as they grouped together, "we let them into it a bit towards the break. We need to press them back again, like we did at the start."

She paused to take a gulp of water, and Jenny piped up. "Hey don't forget – a clean sheet wins us the group. A draw is all we need you know."

Holly's dark eyes flashed with annoyance. That was the wrong thing to say, she thought. Others, though, had quickly latched on to the notion. Comments of "Yeah, if they don't score we're through," and "We've just got to keep it tight at the back," were bringing nods from the other players. Holly was about to challenge this defensive thinking when the referee interrupted. She wanted to start again, because the tournament was running late. Holly never had the chance to explain her views properly.

The danger signs were there almost as soon as the second half began. Earlier, players had been pressing forward, forcing United on to the back foot. Now, too many Amazon players were content to sit back and hold their positions. United, with more of the ball, began to build momentum. One move ended with a shot which just cleared Jenny's crossbar. They were clearly taking control. "We've got to push up more," Holly urged the defence and midfield. "Sitting back is just playing into their hands!"

It was practically a prediction. A minute later, despite Holly's pleas, too many players stayed deep during an Amazon attack, which petered out through lack of support. United swept forward. Defenders backed further and further away. When she reached shooting range, the ball-carrier let fly. Mel Sullivan half-blocked the shot but the ball spun up off her leg, curved away from a stranded Jenny York, and looped into the net. The United players mobbed the scorer.

A goal up, they were favourites for the three points which would put them top of the group and into the semi-finals.

While Jenny bemoaned the deflection, Holly stood on the edge of the penalty area and shook her head slowly. Part of her wanted to let rip angrily, but she knew that in a crisis, the words "I told you so" were pretty useless. Instead, she began rallying her team-mates. "Get your heads up, Amazons! We're not out of this yet! We've got time to pull this out of the fire if we start playing properly again."

The Amazons responded immediately from the restart. Stung by the goal, everyone doubled their efforts. They were nothing if not fighters. Yet by attacking in numbers, sending players forward from the back, the danger was that a break-away would find Villa stretched defensively. If United scored a crucial second goal, the Amazons would be out of it for sure. United were pressed back, forced to defend around their own penalty area, when suddenly Rebecca mishit a pass. United had the ball and counter-attacked. With only Cassy and Denise at the back, their attackers swept forward. They looked certain to score, but seemingly from nowhere, Chrissie Blake sprinted across to make a desperate match-saving tackle, forcing the ball out of play. In doing so, however, she took another painful blow to her already injured leg. It was impossible for her to continue.

Chrissie had to be helped off, while Antonella, as substi-tute, trotted on to the field. Looking anything but confident, she glanced across to where her father was standing. Holly was at her side in moments. The skilful winger had the ability to trouble the United defence if she could only put her baffling unease about playing while her father was watching behind her. "You can do this," Holly stressed, her own eyes fierce with intensity. "Just focus on the field. The crowd disappears, remember." Antonella slowly nodded. Holly wondered if she had got through to her.

She didn't have long to wait to find out. The Amazons

won back possession from the United throw-in. The ball came to Holly, who turned, twisted to give herself some space, then played a firm pass out to Antonella. With a defender closing her down quickly, touching the ball back to Mel was the obvious easy option for the winger. Instead she dragged the ball away from her opponent with the sole of her boot, spin-turning at the same time, then skipped outside the bemused United player to set off down the wing.

A second defender approached but Antonella's quick feet shifted the ball away from the challenger, who was left tackling thin air as the stringy winger jinked past her. In the end, it took a clumsy foul from a United midfield player to stop her, otherwise Antonella might have gone straight through into the United box. Holly helped pull her team-mate back to her feet.

"Brilliant run, Ant. Let's have more of that. You've got them scared of you." Even as she spoke, Holly sensed her team-mate growing in confidence.

The free kick came to nothing, however, and the worry was that Amazon Villa's resurgence would too, for the minutes were ticking away. United, clinging to the slender lead, had all but given up attacking, while Villa, despite lots of pressing, couldn't find a way through. The referee had begun scrutinizing her watch when a throw-in from Mel Sullivan found Antonella with her back to goal on the corner of the penalty box. She looked to be turning inside, but stepped over the ball, pirouetted, and spun away outside. The move bought her time and space to look up and cross, and she shaped to do so when a defender came sliding across to block. Somehow Antonella checked in the process of crossing, deftly pulling the ball back inside to slip past the grounded defender. She ran on towards the goal, moving the ball to her favoured right foot.

"Shoot! Hit it!" yelled Bev Blake. Two more defenders rushed to her, intent on charging down any attempt at goal.

Antonella again fooled everyone, pulling out of the shot at the last instant, pushing the ball to her left again. The sharp change of direction almost brought her to a dead stop but her next movement was to whip her weaker left foot into the ball. She made perfect contact, powering a curling shot goalwards. The sudden thunderbolt foxed the keeper who couldn't react quickly enough. The ball flashed past her, flying into the net. Antonella threw both arms into the air, yelling at the top of her voice. When jubilant team-mates began to engulf her, she was still yelling. It took the referee quite some time to get everyone back to their positions so that the game could restart. It finished just moments after that and the celebrations began all over again. The brilliant goal, a personal triumph for Antonella, meant the game was a draw, but the Amazons, on seven points, topped the group and had made it to the second phase of the competition. As the players danced and hugged each other on the field, someone found their way from the sidelines to Antonella, hauling her aloft. It was her father, as ecstatic as any of the girls, who was shouting, "It's my daughter! It's my footballer!"

THE GOLDEN GOAL

The morning of Easter Monday was as grey as the shirts worn by the opposition the Amazons were to play in the semi-final. The team were Maybury Mavericks, the team of American girls which included the striker Nina had known back in the States, Annie Devlin. The Mavericks had won Group D with the maximum nine points, scoring fourteen goals in the process.

"Their kit looks drab, but they don't play boring stuff," Nina informed her own team-mates. "Saw them a few times on Saturday. They like going forward, and they're fast and inventive when they do. I know one of their strikers, and believe me, she knows where the net is. We're going to have our work cut out." The girls had arrived early at the sports complex to take a look around the stadium, where the second phase games were to be played. "Well, like the cliché kings on the TV say – 'There're no easy games at this level,'" Della joked, putting on a deep, male voice.

"Maybe," smiled Holly, noting the remaining semi-finalists, "but some might have been easier than others." The two other teams to qualify were Dempsey's Diamonds from Group A, and Tilston All-Stars from Group B. "If we'd drawn the All-Stars, we'd have beaten them this time, I'm sure of it," she added. "They only just scraped through their group – one win, two draws. On paper, they're the weakest of the four of us."

"Ah, but as we all know, Des," mocked Della, persisting with her soccer pundit impression, "soccer's not played on paper." Everyone fell about laughing.

"What did you do?" asked Holly, when she'd recovered. "Eat a book of soccer quotes for breakfast or something!" Secretly, though, she was pleased that Della was keeping everyone entertained and relaxed, preventing tensions getting to the players too soon.

The Diamonds v All-Stars game was the first to be played. It went pretty much as Holly expected, with Sandra Dempsey's powerful players taking control almost from the start. The quicksilver centre forward for the Diamonds – who had scored so many against the Amazons – was again in fine form, completing a hat-trick just after half-time. The All-Stars did create one or two chances late in the game when their opponents eased off, only to find an agile keeper blocking the way, determined to prevent them scoring. At the final whistle, it was 6-0 to the Diamonds.

With a gap of half-an-hour between the semi-finals, the Amazons were able to watch the entire game before. During that time, Holly put a lot of thought into how they should approach the match against the Mavericks. She outlined her ideas to Nina and Della first. To begin with, Nina was not convinced at all, but was eventually won over. Then, in the confines of the changing room, Holly addressed the whole team.

"OK, it's like this. Between us and a showdown with the Diamonds are the Mavericks – and their record shows they're a bit tasty. On top of that, there doesn't seem much point in playing ourselves to a standstill to get past the Mavericks if we don't have anything left for the last match. The Diamonds would love that, wouldn't they? They've got the benefit of a longer rest over whoever gets through anyway. Now, if we're going to have any chance today, we've got to get our tactics right. And here's what we've come up with . . ."

The Villa side which kicked off against the Mavericks wasn't radically different from previous games, but its formation and objectives were. Rebecca Fuller was in from the start, as were Antonella and Chrissie Blake. The unlucky player left as sub was Chrissie's sister Bev. She wasn't thrilled, but accepted it when Holly stressed to her that she would be on at some point.

The formation was different because Nina was left to play up front on her own. Rebecca was playing deeper, making five in midfield. Chances for the Amazons would be few and far between, everyone realized that, but the name of the game was containment. The idea was to frustrate and stifle the attacking play of their opponents by denying the dangerous Annie Devlin and her striker-partner as much of the ball as possible. If moves could be broken up early, in the crowded midfield, the Mavericks' forwards would have fewer chances to score themselves. Just as important, this limited, unambitious game-plan was not a physically tiring one.

To a large extent, the tactics went against Holly's own instincts about the game. Yet by half-time, the Mavericks had created just one shooting chance – which Jenny York had saved comfortably – and Holly believed more than ever that the tactics were right for the situation. Nina was not so sure.

"I gotta have more support," she complained. "You lot in midfield, there's five of you. Someone's gotta break out quicker."

Nina had endured a lonely struggle up front. Instead of running on to passes towards goal, she'd found herself receiving the ball with her back to it most of the time. Once in possession, with no partner alongside her, she was also having to keep the ball, fending off defenders as best she could, until her team-mates came forward from their deep positions.

"You're doing brilliant, Nina," Holly enthused quickly. "You're holding the ball so well. We'll get to you as soon as we can, I promise."

"So what, more of the same?" grumbled the frustrated American.

"Until we change and bring on Bev, yeah," insisted Della firmly. "Hang in there, girl. It's working, honest it is."

It continued to work in the second half. The Mavericks, their normal style so effectively disrupted, were finding it difficult to create any openings. If they did get beyond the crowded midfield, they ran straight into the Amazon defence, where Della in particular was in dominating form.

With ten minutes left, and the game still goalless, the Mavericks made a change. A defender was substituted, an extra midfield player taking her place. "Crunch time," Holly confided to Della. "They're trying 3-5-2. Evening up the numbers in the middle, they're leaving just three back to look after Nina. If we go for it right now, before they've sorted themselves out . . ."

Della didn't need to hear any more. "Bev," she yelled. "Get ready!"

It took a few minutes before they could make their own change, but when they did, Bev replaced her sister, who was beginning to feel her injury from Saturday. The team reverted to its normal 4-4-2 formation. The bold move was to suddenly pit two up against an unsuspecting three, when for most of the game it had been just Nina against a familiar and comfortable back four.

The hoped-for confusion came when Holly stretched to win a sliding tackle in midfield, bounced up to side-step a second Maverick player and advanced at pace. With Bev and Nina just in front of her, and the opposition back-line retreating, it was three against three. The ball at her feet, the best chance of the game was unfolding before Holly.

Nina peeled to the left, Bev the right. The uncertain

defenders were all at sea. Suddenly, Nina knifed back in towards goal and Holly struck her a pass. It bisected two defenders to fall perfectly into Nina's stride. She touched it forward. The third defender hurtled across, diving in front of Nina. She was waiting for it, checked, nudged the ball to her right and rounded the flailing, grounded defender. The Mavericks' keeper raced off her line. Nina saw her coming, pushed the ball further right to give herself an angle, then pivoted and shot, falling back as she connected. Rising, the ball flew towards the empty goal. Then flew over it.

On her back on the ground, Nina let out a screaming roar. Holly appeared, dragging her to her feet. "That was it!" wailed Nina, putting her head in her hands. "We've spent the whole game working for that! Setting up that one chance to put us in the final! And I blew it!"

"Hey, lay off yourself," Holly told her. "No one's worked harder than you to make this game-plan work. You're the one who's had to play a different role most of the time." She playfully ruffled her team-mate's hair. "You'll forget all about this miss when you score the winner." Nina grunted again. She was still angry at herself, but Holly could see the fierce resolve in her eyes. She knew Nina would be OK.

Without a further chance for either side, the game moved into extra time – a period when, if one team scored, it would be a Golden Goal, and the game would finish immediately. If no goal was scored, the winners would be decided by a penalty shoot-out.

The nerve-wracking period began with the team of American girls on top. They had the extra player in midfield now, and began carving out chances. One fell to Annie Devlin, who raced clear only to hit a powerful shot wide of the goal. A minute later, the second Mavericks forward outran Cassy to shoot low across Jenny York. She dived and fingertipped the ball away. From the clearance, the Amazons counter-attacked. Nina, her confidence unaffected after the miss, collected a pass from Antonella, cut inside a defender and played a searching ball forward for Bev. Her first-time shot was clawed away by the keeper for a corner. The tight, cautious regular-time game had evolved into a thrilling, open encounter with chances coming at both ends.

For the first time in the match, Della trotted forward for the corner. Antonella hit a curling, inswinging cross into the heart of the penalty area. Della outjumped everyone. She met the ball firmly, her header bulleting toward the goal. The keeper dived. A defender on the goal-line jumped up. Both missed the ball – it flashed into the net. "Goooaaalll!" screamed every Amazon player.

They came from all angles, hurling themselves at the shrieking goalscorer, yelling and hollering themselves. The heaving scrum collapsed as more bodies threw themselves onto the pile. Someone said afterwards that it was a good job it had been Della, for no one else was big and strong enough to withstand the ensuing melee that engulfed the scorer. Eventually they peeled away, twos and threes still clinging to each other. Nina found Holly and threw her arms around her, planting a joyous kiss on the top of her head. "You genius! You little genius! What a tactician!" They embraced some more, then turned to find Annie Devlin approaching them. She looked hugely disappointed, but stretched out a hand.

"Well done. You guys played one heck of a smart game."

Holly shook hands, then Nina gave her compatriot a hug. "Sorry, Annie," she whispered. The blonde girl shrugged.

"Hey, can't win if you can't lose. Just make sure you guys win the final, y'hear?"

CHAPTER FOURTEEN

GOAL POWER

There was a forty-five minute break before the final. The Amazons spent the time recharging on energy drinks and foods like bananas, and stretching to keep their muscles warm. They'd played conservatively for most of the semi-final, and the Golden Goal had been scored quite early in extra time, so no one felt overly tired. The only problem was Chrissie Blake. Her leg was sore despite repeated applications of fiery muscle-rub ointment. She felt OK to start the game, but no one expected her to finish it.

"Cuts down our options," Holly told the others, "but there's a couple of things which could work for us. First, they've just watched us play very defensively. They're probably thinking we'll play the same way again, because – second – they hammered us 13-0 last time. We're a soft touch to them. There's a chance they'll be complacent, expecting another easy game."

"Starting to figure how your mind works," said Nina. "You want us to blitz them hard from the off, catch them cold."

"Bit like the Sloneton Rangers game on Saturday?" suggested Della, and Holly nodded. "Yeah. Let's give 'em a wake up call they'll never forget," the captain smiled, relishing the prospect.

The Amazons tore at the Diamonds from the first whistle. Holly and Vickie snapped at their opposite numbers in midfield, who began with several casual passes. Vickie intercepted one and quickly fed Antonella out wide. The Villa winger teased the full back in front of her with feints to go inside, then outside. The defender stretched to tackle, but was foxed again as Antonella slipped the ball through the gap between the full back's legs.

Nipping inside her floundering opponent, Antonella was on to the ball again in a flash. With space in front of her, she had time to look up. A central defender was rushing out to confront her, leaving Nina unmarked. The Villa winger picked out her team-mate with a precise pass. Nina controlled the ball, turned and shot all in one smooth, flowing movement. The ball arrowed towards the corner of the net. Hurling herself across her line, the Diamonds keeper just got a hand to the ball. Her startling save deflected the shot on to the post. The ball bounced back into play, but before Bev could pounce, the keeper was up swiftly to grab the rebound. Immediately, she looked for a team-mate with a quick throw-out. The player wasn't ready to take possession, however. She failed to control the ball, letting it run out of play. The Diamonds looked unsettled.

Quite a crowd had gathered for the match. The Diamonds were strong favourites, but many of those watching warmed to the encouraging start made by the underdogs. The vocal support increased as the Amazons attacked again. Once more the move built down the right, this time with Antonella playing a neat one-two with Holly. The winger advanced, but instead of crossing, she squared the ball back inside again to Holly. A defender blocked her shot, though the ricochet ran through to Bev. Her effort was beaten away by another diving stop from the keeper. Nina scrambled for the rebound, squeezing between two defenders to make contact. She caught just enough of the ball to prod it home. It wasn't the prettiest of goals, but it gave the Amazons a shock early lead.

The robust start of their opponents had shaken the Diamonds to their boots. Initially over-confident, they were thrown out of their stride completely by the goal. They were almost caught again several minutes later, when only a point-blank save by their busy goalkeeper prevented Bev adding to the lead.

For the Amazons, no one was playing better than Holly. She was everywhere. Her tireless running was backed up by crisp tackling and top-quality passing. When he'd played well, Holly had heard her father talk about "being in the zone" – about moving to exactly the right place or playing exactly the right pass almost before thinking about the action concerned. Holly had struck similar form at the perfect time. She and her team-mates kept the Diamonds at bay, even during the later part of the first half when they came more into the match.

At the break, the Amazons gestured encouragingly at each other. Geeing one another along, they all kept focussed, kept their feet on the ground. No one needed telling that the Diamonds, receiving an audible roasting from Sandra Dempsey, would throw everything at them from the restart. Yet the incentive to hold them at bay was enormous; they were just one half away from the Women's World Cup. "We could go back to five in midfield," suggested Denise Lambert. "Contain them, protect our lead."

"Uh-uh. Sorry girls, I don't think that's an option," answered Chrissie, wincing. "I struggled a bit, those last few minutes. It's better if Becs comes on for me. The pressure they're going to put us under, we'll need everyone fit out there."

The substitution was a straight swap, with Rebecca lining up in Chrissie's place in midfield at the start of the second half. The Diamonds began it aggressively. Their determination to get back on level terms brought some over-physical challenges. A towering central defender, the one who took their goal-kicks, usually booming them straight into the Amazon half, put in a heavy tackle on Nina. The foul earned the player a rebuke from the referee, but shook up the American striker for several minutes. Soon after, Holly received a painful wrap on the ankle from another foul tackle.

"They're out to rough us up," Holly called to her team-mates, loud enough for their opponents to hear. "Shows how desperate they are. Just stand firm girls, let them know we can't be intimidated."

At that point, the referee addressed both sets of players. She stressed she wouldn't hesitate to send off anyone deliberately flouting the laws of the game.

While they remained competitive, the rough stuff from the Diamonds stopped after that. They began to play much better than in the first half, too. Some of the superior skills they possessed, which had helped them humiliate the Amazons in their previous match, started to show through. Holly and Vickie, working like demons to break up moves in the middle of the field, were being stretched. All four members of the Villa back-line had to make crucial interceptions or win vital tackles to prevent the red-and-white-shirted strikers getting in on goal.

Midway through the half, Mel Sullivan made another important challenge just outside the penalty area and seemed to have won the ball fairly when the referee whistled for a foul. The harsh decision gave the Diamonds a free kick in a dangerous area. Nina and Bev were called back to help defend. With so many players in front of her, Jenny York had difficulty seeing what was happening. But it was very simple. A Diamonds player pushed the freekick to one side into space, the strong-looking centre back steamed forward, hit a thunderous shot, and a split-second later, with Jenny rooted to the ground, the ball was in the back of the net. The Diamonds were level.

Before Holly could say anything, Vickie began shouting encouragement to lift the team. "All right Amazons, let's get straight back into it. We had this lot on the back foot before, and we can do it again." Others chipped in with more rallying words, which gave Holly real hope. She felt the spirit among the players – the determination to keep plugging away no matter what set-backs befell them – was fantastic. They believed they could still win against these technically better players, and Holly believed it too.

That resolve helped them carry the game right back at the Diamonds. Almost from the restart, Antonella fashioned an opening for Bev who shot fractionally the wrong side of a post. Soon after, a strong tackle from Vickie diverted the ball square to Holly. She glanced up, saw Nina making a forward run, and lifted a lovely pass over the big centre back for her team-mate to chase. Only the alertness of the opposition goalkeeper, racing from her line and bravely diving at the striker's feet to smother the ball on the edge of her penalty area, prevented further danger.

The keeper followed that save with another swift throw-out. She found her right full back, who instantly moved the ball up the line, and suddenly the Diamonds were counter-attacking. Alarm bells rang in Holly's head. She sprinted back downfield, striving to provide extra cover. As happened many times in the first encounter, slick passing from the Diamonds opened up the Amazons on their left. When a hard, low cross came over, a searing burst of pace put the lightening-quick striker a vital step ahead of Della and Cassy. She stretched and found the perfect touch on the ball to flick it wide of Jenny's dive. The best move of the match had put the Diamonds 2-1 ahead.

Within minutes, the game had swung cruelly against the Amazons. Several of them sank to their knees. Faces that reflected determination following the first goal now showed despair.

"Nothing anyone could do," said Della, shaking her head. "Just a top goal. Come on, Amazons!" She didn't mean it to be, but the captain's attempt to lift her players was full of desperation. Holly, gasping in lungfuls of air after chasing back, wondered if the spirit which had carried them so far had finally been broken. Suddenly she felt very tired.

When the game kicked-off again, the Diamonds seemed quicker in all parts of the field. They had a firm grip on the game, and didn't look like they would ever let go. Holly chased and covered as best she could, yet had to watch them string a dozen passes together before anyone got close enough to challenge. More passes zipped across the field before Holly slid in to make an interception, succeeding only in knocking the ball straight into the perimeter stand. A spectator caught it. When he stepped forward to lob the ball back, Holly recognized him. It was Mr Peterson, the coach from the Soccer Fun course. So much had happened since then, she reflected. Even Duncan Ramsey, who'd wanted to cause her trouble on that course, had changed his tune. "Some girls can kick after all," he'd said when last they'd met.

Holly slapped a hand hard on her thigh. She was losing concentration, she needed to snap back into focus. The Diamonds took their throw-in. A fast drag-back and turn from the player collecting the ball fooled Vickie, who challenged late and up-ended her tormentor. Vickie raised her hand in apology, while the referee called to the sidelines for someone to attend the injured player.

"Game's getting away from us, Hol," remarked an anxious-looking Nina during the brief hold up. "We can't even get a kick. How we gonna pull this back?"

Over Nina's shoulder, Holly saw the Diamonds keeper jigging about on the edge of her penalty area, staying alert. Holly stared at the keeper. While she did, it seemed to Holly that two phrases which had just passed through her mind collided and became jumbled up, leaving only a few words which made any sense. "Some girls . . . can't even . . . kick . . ." was all she could understand. Holly's eyes narrowed. "Listen," she heard herself saying to Nina, "listen . . ."

From the freekick, the Diamonds worked another good shooting chance which was put narrowly wide. The Amazons were hanging on by their fingernails.

A minute later, another quick move down the right was broken up by Rebecca, who found Holly with a pass inside. She had Antonella in space on the right, yet instead launched a long, slightly desperate-looking ball forward behind the Diamonds' back-line. Nina gave chase, although the defender had turned and wasn't going to be beaten to the ball. She directed a pass back precisely towards her goalkeeper who, under the rules, wasn't able to use her hands. Immediately, as Holly had suggested, Nina visibly accelerated. Running hard, the Amazon forward was aware of a Diamonds full back moving into space to give the keeper a straightforward passing option. Yet as the American homed in on her target, the keeper hesitated. When she didn't play the pass first time, but trapped the ball with an uncertain touch instead, Nina knew there was a chance. The keeper had to step back to give herself room before attempting to steer the ball wide to her team-mate. Nina threw out a leg. She caught the ball with the sole of her boot, knocking it down into her own path. She was after it and on to it in a trice. One touch brought the ball under her control, a second curled it straight into the centre of the empty net. It was all-square again, at 2-2.

Running back after congratulating the scorer, the Amazon players waved clenched fists at each other. The word about the goalkeeper's weakness spread amongst them like whispered gossip. "She can't kick! Their keeper can't kick!"

"How'd you know, Hol?" grinned Nina.

"Left the goal-kicks to the centre back. Only ever threw it out. I just couldn't remember ever seeing her kick – and let's face it, we were desperate!"

"Not any more!" roared Della.

There were five minutes left. The Amazons had an edge, had momentum. The Diamonds, despite their superior skill, were suddenly vulnerable. Their defenders looked nervous every time one of them received the ball, knowing the "safety first" pass back to the keeper was too dangerous an option now. They hit hurried passes forward, invariably giving possession straight back to the Amazons. Sandra Dempsey on the touch-line became more and more agitated. "Hold the ball! Hold the ball!" she implored. "We can't build attacks if we keep giving it away!"

Their tails up, the Amazons pressed at every opportunity. When the opposition left back received the ball, and tried to follow her coach's instructions, Antonella was in to snap at her heels. The full back wriggled free from the winger, but Mel Sullivan charged forward too and whisked the ball away. She made ground before crossing for Nina just inside the penalty area. She swivelled and shot on the turn, only for her marker to block the effort.

The ball came out to Holly. She seemed set to shoot first time, but with defenders racing towards her she caressed the ball lightly to her right, clearing the first challenger, glancing goalwards at the same time. The keeper had moved forward, setting herself up for the expected shot. Holly went for it. Her chip shot rose, then dipped in a long, graceful arc. The ball cleared the outstretched hands of the keeper, throwing herself up and back, to pass under the crossbar and into the net. Dempsey's Diamonds 2 Amazon Villa 3.

The three minutes until the final whistle seemed like three hours for the Amazons. One mighty scramble in front of Jenny York ended with a corner, which Cassy headed clear. The ball fell to the powerful centre back who'd scored earlier. She smashed it with everything she had and, to every Amazon's relief, sent it high over the bar. Once the goal-kick was taken, the ref blew for full time.

"Yes! Yes! Yes!" screamed Holly, punching the air with both arms before Nina, Antonella and Bev wrapped their arms around her. Vickie and Rebecca grabbed each other, dancing round and round. When Chrissie Blake hobbled over to join them, the three toppled over. "Ow! That hurts," Chrissie laughed uncontrollably, clutching at her injury, "that really hurts!"

Cassy's mother embraced her daughter, who looked like she couldn't quite believe it all. Mel's brother Roy hoisted his sister high into the air. "Better start clearing some space on the shelves for my soccer medals now," she beamed.

Della and Jenny clung on to each other's shoulders and screamed in each other's faces. They only stopped when Denise Lambert appeared alongside them, tears streaming down her face. Between great heaving sobs she managed to say, "I'm so happy."

Holly turned when she became aware of someone tapping her shoulder. It was Sandra Dempsey. "Congratulations, Holly. I see I was wrong about your team-mates. They make more than a decent team. Wasn't wrong about you though. Well played. Learn what you can from your trip."

"Thanks. I will," replied Holly. She turned back to the gathering, triumphant Amazon Villa players, declaring, "Women's World Cup, here we come!"

SECOND HALF

The FIFA Women's World Cup

The third FIFA Women's World Cup tournament will be played in the USA in the summer of 1999. The tournament's opening ceremony and its first game are scheduled for June 19, 1999. The final takes place on July 10, 1999.

Previous tournaments, held in China in 1991 and Sweden four years later, were contested by 12 countries, but the competition has now expanded, with 16 nations set to take part.

Women's World Cup '99 Draw

On February 14, 1999, the draw took place allocating the qualifying nations to groups for the first round. Four countries – USA, Germany, Norway and China – were seeded to head each group.

Group A – USA, North Korea, Nigeria, Denmark.
Group B – Germany, Brazil, Mexico, Italy.
Group C – Norway, Japan, Canada, Russia.
Group D – China, Australia, Ghana, Sweden.

Qualifying Highlights

Norway are the defending Champions. However, that status did not earn an automatic qualification for this tournament. The Norwegians had to battle through the qualifying process, which started in August 1997 and featured more than 60 other nations.

Norway were drawn in one of the most competitive European groups, along with England, Germany and Holland. It was very closely contested as eight of the 12 qualifying games were won by a single goal, while another finished all-square. And in the latter stages of the qualifying process, it was only narrow defeats to the World Champions – by the odd goal in three at home, and 2-0 away – which effectively ended England's hopes of progressing.

The Oceania qualifying tournament took place in Auckland, New Zealand in October, 1998. Australia, Fiji, New Zealand, Papua New Guinea, Tonga and Western Samoa took part. As in the two previous qualifying tournaments, Australia met New Zealand in the final. It was the Matilders of Australia who waltzed past their regional rivals, recording a 3-1 victory to claim a second successive World Cup qualification. Though officially placed 12th and last in the 1995 World Cup, the Matilders are expected to do better in the USA. Women's soccer in Australia is benefiting from increased resources because of the approaching year 2000 Olympic Games, to be held in Sydney.

Canada powered through the Confederation of North and Central America and Caribbean Football (CONCACAF) qualifying tournament, scoring 42 goals and conceding none in five matches. A 1-0 victory in the final against Mexico gave the Canadians an automatic qualification place, leaving the defeated Mexicans to contest a play-off against Argentina, runners-up behind Brazil in the South American qualifying competition. Held over two legs, Mexico triumphed both at home and in Argentina to clinch the last of the 16 places for the 1999 Finals.

Tournament Structure And Venues

In the first round, the four teams in each group play each other once, making a total of 24 matches. The top two sides from each group progress to the quarter-finals, when the tournament becomes a straight knockout competition. At this stage, if the scores are level after 90 minutes, the game moves into "Golden Goal" extra time - as experienced by Holly and Amazon Villa in the story. Extra time lasts for two 15-minute periods unless a goal is scored, at which point the game ends immediately. If no Golden Goal is scored, the winner will be determined by a penalty shoot-out. The four winning teams from the quarter-finals go forward to play in the semi-finals. The winners of those meet in the final, while the losing semi-finalists contest the third place match. A total of 32 games will be played in all.

The opening game of this Women's World Cup is scheduled to feature host nation USA v Denmark, at the Giants Stadium, New York, New Jersey. The final is set for the Rose Bowl in Pasadena. Across the country, eight stadia in seven areas will stage games. They are:

Foxboro Stadium, Boston – 5 games
Soldier Field, Chicago – 4 games
Rose Bowl, Pasadena – 4 games
Giants Stadium, New York/New Jersey – 4 games
Civic Stadium, Portland – 4 games
Spartan Stadium, San Francisco/San Jose – 4 games
Stanford Stadium, San Francisco/San Jose – 1 game
Jack Kent Cooke Stadium, Washington – 6 games

Women's World Cup History

The first Women's World Cup took place in China in 1991. From the 12 countries involved, the USA played Norway in the final. A crowd of 63,000 watched the game, with the Americans coming out on top by 2-1. Striker Michelle Akers scored both goals, the second coming late in the game. Akers finished as the tournament's leading scorer with 10 goals, out of her country's total of 25, from 6 games. New Zealand, representing Oceania, were eliminated at the group stage; England did not qualify.

The Women's World Cup of 1995 was played in Sweden. Again, 12 countries took part, and again, Norway reached the final, this time with Germany providing the opposition. The runners-up from 1991 went one better this time, earning the title World Champions with a 2-0 victory. In six games, Norway scored 23 times and conceded just one goal. A crowd of more than 17,000 watched the final. It was broadcast live by 16 countries, including Norway, where an estimated one in three of the population witnessed their country's triumph. The USA finished third, while England were eliminated in the quarter-finals, and Australia went out at the group stage.

Women's Soccer at the Olympics

There is another global international women's soccer tournament, and that is at the Olympic Games. The 1996 Olympics in Atlanta saw women's soccer included as a demonstration sport. The final was fought out between the USA and China. The host nation took the gold medal with a 2-1 victory, in front of an incredible 76,000 spectators.

Qualification for the Olympics went to the eight countries which reached the quarter-final stage of the 1995 Women's World Cup. This included England, knocked out at that stage by eventual finalists Germany. However, as it is Great Britain, not its component nations, which takes part in the Olympics, England's women soccer players had to miss out. Their place went to Brazil, officially placed ninth at the 1995 World Cup. The stand-ins, though, finished a very creditable fourth at the Atlanta Olympics. Quite how well England might have done if allowed to compete, we will never know.

As in 1995, teams reaching the quarter-finals of the 1999 World Cup will then qualify for the women's soccer tournament at the year 2000 Olympics in Sydney.

Girls' and Women's Soccer In the USA

FIFA has estimated that there 30 million female soccer players world-wide. In 1994, it was calculated that six million American females participated in the sport, the largest number in any one nation. Today, some estimates claim as many as nine million girls and women in the States play the game. In a nutshell, girls in America are receiving every encouragement to enjoy soccer. They can be seen playing the game all over the country, just like boys in Britain.

As unlikely as it might sound to an outsider, the strength of women's soccer in America today owes much to a change in the law regarding education. In 1972, Title IX of the Education Acts Amendments outlawed discrimination by sex in federally funded schools. It meant that for every dollar spent on male education, a dollar had to be spent on female education – including on sports programs. With financial resources pouring into female sports at schools, participation levels grew dramatically. Before the 1972 Amendment approximately 300,000 girls played inter-school sports, while today, that figure is in the region of two-and-a-quarter million.

With more and more school-aged girls playing soccer throughout the 1970s, the next rung of the education system, the colleges, began to offer soccer programs for female students. The numbers of programs mushroomed throughout the next two decades, as did inter-college competition. In 1999, formal competition is run by the National Collegiate

Athletics Association, with colleges ranked in either Divisions I, II, or III. Division I and II colleges can offer students soccer scholarships, and quite a number of players from abroad, including from Britain, have been granted them.

Division I college soccer receives a lot of press and TV coverage because, until recently, it was the highest level of competition available. The lack of a club league structure of a similar standard was seen as a problem, for players leaving college had no real place to go. However, the recent creation of the W-League, America's first national adult women's soccer league, addressed this issue.

Starting with just eight teams in 1994 as a test scheme, the 1998 season saw more than 30 teams competing in the W-1 and W-2 Leagues. Several teams fielded players in contention for a place in the current USA World Cup side, including Brandi Chastain, Julie Foudy, Christie Pearce and Sara Whalen. Perhaps the biggest name in the League, though, was Michelle Akers, who signed to play for Tampa Bay Extreme.

Other top sides include former W-League Champions Maryland Pride and Long Island Lady Riders. Champions of W-1 League in 1998 were Raleigh Wings, triumphing from the following three division structure:

W-1 North Div	W-1 Central Div	W-1 South Div
Boston Renegades	Buffalo Ffillies	Atlanta Classics
Delaware Genies	Chicago Cobras	Charlotte Speed
Long Island Lady Riders	Columbus Ziggx	Jackson Calypso
Maryland Pride	Denver Diamonds	Raleigh Wings
New Jersey Wildcats	Rochester Ravens	Tampa Bay Extreme

The hope for the future is that the Women's World Cup will generate sufficient interest to allow the W-League to grow into a fully professional national league.

What's a Girl Gotta Do if She Wants to Play?

Do you want to give girls' soccer a try? Well, one way of getting started is to contact a US youth soccer organization. There are several of these, but by far the largest is the United States Youth Soccer Association (USYSA). It is made up of 55 member State Associations (some States have two) and has over three million registered players between the ages of five and nineteen. The USYSA provides programs aimed at meeting the needs of all kids. So if you want to play just for fun, or if you are looking for a more skilled, competitive level, they'll be able to help you. You can contact USYSA by calling 1-800 4 SOCCER. The full postal address is:

USYSA
899 Presidential Drive
Suite # 117
Richardson, Texas 75081

You can e-mail them too at: usysoccer@aol.com
There is also a website: http://www.usysa.org/

Once you've made contact, the USYSA will put you in touch with your local State Association, which will be able to give you the information you need on the programs and teams in your area.

Should you find the sheer size and scope of the USYSA too daunting, and you are more interested in giving soccer a try on a recreational basis first, the much smaller Soccer Association for Youth (SAY) might be more to your liking. SAY concentrates its efforts on the fun side of soccer, providing opportunities for all children between four and eighteen, no matter what their size or ability, to take part in the sport. SAY has no State Associations, so members and leagues deal directly with its national headquarters. You can call them on 1-800-233-7291. The full postal address is:

Soccer Association For Youth, USA
4050 Executive Park Drive
Suite 100
Cincinnati, Oh 45241

Their e-mail number is: SAYUSA@aol.com
Their website is: http://www.saysoccer.org/
Both USYSA and SAY are non-profit organizations, and both are affiliated to the United States Soccer Federation, the governing body of the sport in the country.

Girls' and Women's Soccer in the UK

Interest in girls' and women's soccer in the UK is currently growing at an astonishing rate. But females really began playing the game to a high level as long ago as the First World War. During that conflict, the role of women in society began to alter. A number of women's teams came into being around that period, playing games which raised funds for charity.

The most famous side to appear at that time played under the name of Dick, Kerr Ladies. It was formed by women workers at W.B. Dick and John Kerr's engineering factory in Preston. They were there because so many of the male workforce had left for the army. They played many games at Preston's Deepdale ground, and at a number of other grounds owned by professional clubs, attracting some very large crowds. On Boxing Day in 1920, some 53,000 were at Everton's Goodison Park ground to see Dick, Kerr Ladies beat St Helens Ladies 4-0.

Almost 12 months later, however, the Football Association banned women from playing on Football League grounds. The FA declared in its statement: ". . . the game of football is quite unsuitable for females . . ." Women's soccer did continue, but attendances fell, interest waned, and the number of teams sharply declined.

A resurgence did not occur until after the men's England team won the World Cup in 1966. Soccer enjoyed a "golden era" in that period, and by late 1969, with growing female interest in the sport, the Women's Football Association was formed with 44 member clubs. Two years later, the FA had lifted its ban on women playing on the grounds of its affiliated clubs, the Union of European Football Associations (UEFA) had recommended that National Associations should take control of all soccer, and the first Women's FA Cup competition was won by Southampton.

Two decades later, in 1991, the WFA was strong enough to launch a National League. It consisted of 24 clubs, eight each in a Premier Division, a Northern Division and a Southern Division. The Doncaster Belles were the first Premier Division Champions. They completed a "double" by capturing the WFA Cup in the same season, too.

The Belles are one of a number of clubs which are totally independent. Others, such as Wembley and Croydon, are associated with non-League men's clubs. Many more of the top women's teams, though, have links with professional men's clubs. Arsenal, Liverpool, Everton and Millwall are some examples.

The FA, having already taken control of WFA Cup, renaming it the FA Women's Challenge Cup, assumed responsibility for organization and administration of the Women's National League in 1994. Now called the Football Association Women's Premier League, it has expanded to 10 teams in each division.

For the 1998-99 season the FAWPL National Division is made up of the following teams:

FAWPL National Division

Arsenal	Ilkeston Town
Bradford City	Liverpool
Croydon	Millwall Lionesses
Doncaster Belles	Southampton Saints
Everton	Tranmere Rovers

So . . . Fancy a Game?

Do you want to give girls' soccer a try? You'll be joining one of the fastest growing sports for females if you do. In 1990, the same year in which the English Schools Football Association changed its rules to allow mixed competitive soccer in schools up to the age of 11, there were just 80 all-girl teams. In 1998, there were over 1,000, with some 20,000 players.

The great thing about it is that girls' soccer is now structured so that you can play just for fun, or more seriously, all the way up to senior level, if you want to. To learn how you can get involved, and find out about the teams in your area, you can write to:

Women's Football Co-ordinator
The Football Association
9 Wyllyotts Place
Potters Bar
Herts EN6 2JD

Or, you can phone the Women's Football Hotline on: 01707 647 250.

The Last Word

At the 1995 Women's World Cup, the success of the tournament led FIFA to state that "The future is feminine."

You could be part of that future. If you've never done so before, why not give soccer a try? All you really need is little bit of space and a ball. Can you kick it? Sure you can – and you've got the world at your feet!

FOUR-FOUR-TWO FORMATION

Four defenders, four midfielders, and two attackers – or 4-4-2.
This is the most common line-up in soccer. In all formations, there
is flexibility during play in that, for example, a defender may surge
forward to attack, while a midfield player can drop back to cover the
defender's position.

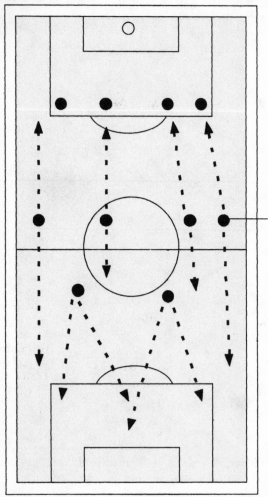

The wide midfield
players are
effectively
wingers when the
team attacks.

Midfield players
cover the length of
the field,
supporting in
attack and helping
defence.